5 DIGITAL SAT
MATH PRACTICE TESTS

AMERICAN MATH
ACADEMY

By H. TONG, M.Ed.

Math Instructional & Olympiad Coach
www.americanmathacademy.com

AMERICAN MATH ACADEMY

5 DIGITAL SAT MATH PRACTICE TESTS

Writer: H.Tong
Copyright © 2023 The American Math Academy LLC.

All rights reserved. No part of this publication may be reproduced in whole or in part, stored in a retrieval system, or transmitted in any form or by any means electronic, mechanical, photocopying, recording or otherwise, without written permission of the copyright owner.

Printed in United States of America.

ISBN: 9798399980263

SAT is registered trademark of the College Entrance Examination Board, which is not involved in the production of, and does not endorse, this product.

Although the writer has made every effort to ensure the accuracy and completeness of information contained this book, the writer assumes no responsibility for errors, inaccuracies, omissions or any inconsistency herein. Any slighting of people, places, or organizations unintentional.

Questions, suggestions or comments, please email: americanmathacademy@gmail.com

TABLE OF CONTENTS

Digital SAT Math Sample Questions---1-7

Math Practice Test I--8-24

Math Practice Test I Solutions--25-38

Math Practice Test II--39-55

Math Practice Test II Solutions---56-67

Math Practice Test III---68-85

Math Practice Test III Solutions--86-98

Math Practice Test IV--99-115

Math Practice Test IV Solutions---116-128

Math Practice Test V--129-144

Math Practice Test V Solutions---145-157

About the Author

Mr. Tong teaches at various private and public schools in both New York and New Jersey. In conjunction with his teaching, Mr. Tong developed his own private tutoring company. His company developed a unique way of ensuring their students' success on the math section of the SAT. His students, over the years, have been able to apply the knowledge and skills they learned during their tutoring sessions in college and beyond. Mr. Tong's academic accolades make him the best candidate to teach SAT Math. He received his master's degree in Math Education. He has won several national and state championships in various math competitions and has taken his team to victory in the Olympiads. He has trained students for Math Counts, American Math Competition (AMC), Harvard MIT Math Tournament, Princeton Math Contest, and the National Math League, and many other events. His teaching style ensures his students' successhe personally invests energy and time into his students and sees what and what they're struggling with. His dedication towards his students is evident through his students' achievements.

Acknowledgements

I would like to take the time to acknowledge the help and support of my beloved wife, my colleagues, and my students–their feedback on my book was invaluable. I would like to say an additional thank you to my dear friend Robert for his assistance in making this book complete. Without everyone's help, this book would not be the same. I dedicate this book to my precious daughter Vera, my inspiration to take on this project.

DIGITAL SAT MATH SAMPLE QUESTIONS

Question #1

If $3x - ay + 12 = 0$ and the slope of the equation is $\frac{3}{4}$, then what is the value of a?

A) 4

B) $\frac{1}{4}$

C) 2

D) $\frac{1}{2}$

Solution:

$3x - ay + 12 = 0$ and $m = \frac{3}{4}$

Slope of equation : $m = \frac{3}{a}$

$\frac{3}{a} = \frac{3}{4}$, then $a = 4$

Correct Answer : A

Question #2

If $x - 3y = 3$, then find $\frac{2^x}{8^y}$

A) 4

B) 8

C) 16

D) 32

Solution:

$x - 3y = 3$, then $\frac{2^x}{2^{3y}} = 2^{x-3y} = 2^3 = 8$

Correct Answer : B

Question #3

$x + 3ky = 12$

$5x - 12y = 18$

In the system of equations above, k is a constant. For what value of k will the system of equations have no solutions?

A) $-\frac{4}{5}$

B) $\frac{4}{5}$

C) $\frac{5}{4}$

D) $-\frac{5}{4}$

Solution:

$x + 3ky = 12$

$5x - 12y = 18$

$m_1 = \frac{-1}{3k}$, $m_2 = \frac{+5}{12}$

if a system has no solution, then slopes must be equals.

$m_1 = m_2$

$\frac{-1}{3k} = \frac{+5}{12}$, $15k = -12$

$k = \frac{-12}{15} = \frac{-4}{5}$

Correct Answer : A

DIGITAL SAT MATH SAMPLE QUESTIONS

Question #4

$$\frac{3(x+5)-8}{7} = \frac{17-(6-x)}{5}$$

In the equation above, what is the value of x?

A) $\frac{21}{4}$

B) $\frac{11}{4}$

C) $\frac{4}{21}$

D) $\frac{23}{4}$

Solution:

$$\frac{3x+15-8}{7} = \frac{17-6+x}{5}$$

$$\frac{3x+7}{7} = \frac{11+x}{5} \text{ (Cross multiply)}$$

$$5(3x+7) = 7(11+x)$$

$$15x+35 = 77+7x$$

$$15x-7x = 77-35$$

$$8x = 42$$

$$x = \frac{42}{8} = \frac{21}{4}$$

Correct Answer : A

Question #5

Simplify $\frac{x^2y + xy^2 - xy}{x^2 + xy - x}$

A) x

B) y

C) 2xy

D) −x

Solution:

$$\frac{x^2y + xy^2 - xy}{x^2 + xy - x}$$

$$= \frac{xy(x+y-1)}{x(x+y-1)}$$

$$= \frac{xy}{x} = y$$

Correct Answer : B

Question #6

Which of the following is equal to $\frac{8^2 \cdot 16^3}{2^{10}}$?

A) 2^8

B) 2^7

C) 2^5

D) 2^4

Solution:

$$\frac{8^2 \cdot 16^3}{2^{10}} = \frac{2^6 \cdot 2^{12}}{2^{10}} = \frac{2^{18}}{2^{10}} = 2^8$$

Correct Answer : A

DIGITAL SAT MATH SAMPLE QUESTIONS

Question #7

Mr. Robert is planning to register at Star Fitness. If the center's monthly fee is $25 and $5 per hour, which of following functions gives Mr. Robert the cost, in dollars, for a month in which he spends x hours training?

A) $F(x) = 5x$

B) $F(x) = 25x$

C) $F(x) = 5 + 25x$

D) $F(x) = 25 + 5x$

Solution:

Mounthly Fee = $25

Per hour : $5

Monthly spending : x hours

$F(x) = 25 + 5x$

Correct Answer : D

Question #8

If $x^2 + ax - 10 = (x - 1)(bx + c)$, then find $b + c$.

A) 50

B) 10

C) 11

D) 12

Solution:

$x^2 + ax - 10 = (x-1)(bx + c)$
$x^2 + ax - 10 = bx^2 + cx - bx - c$
$bx^2 = x^2$, $b = 1$
$-10 = -c$, $c = 10$
$b + c = 11$

Correct Answer : C

Question #9

What are the zeros the function $f(x) = x^3 + 8x^2 + 16x$?

A) 0, −2

B) 0, −3

C) 0, −4

D) 0, −5

Solution:

$f(x) = x^3 + 8x^2 + 16x = 0$
$f(x) = x(x^2 + 8x + 16) = 0$
$f(x) = x(x+4)(x+4) = 0$
$x = 0$ or $x + 4 = 0$, $x = -4$

Correct Answer : C

DIGITAL SAT MATH SAMPLE QUESTIONS

Question #10

If the equation $\dfrac{20x^2}{2x-1}$ is written in the form $k + \dfrac{5}{2x-1}$ which of the following gives k in terms of x?

A) $10 - 5x$

B) $10x + 5$

C) $5x + 10$

D) $5x - 10$

Solution:

$$\begin{array}{r} 10x+5 \\ 2x-1\overline{\smash{)}20x^2 } \\ \underline{-20x^2 \pm 10x} \\ 10x \\ \underline{10x \pm 5} \\ 5 \end{array}$$

$k + \dfrac{5}{2x-1} = 10x + 5 + \dfrac{5}{2x-1}$

$k = 10x + 5$

Correct Answer : B

Question #11

If a and b are positive integers and $\sqrt{a} = b^2 = 4$, then which of following is the value of a − b?

A) 0

B) 1

C) 12

D) 14

Solution:

$b \mp 2$ since b is positive then

$b = 2$

$a = 16$

$a - b = 16 - 2 = 14$

Correct Answer : D

Question #12

If $\dfrac{x+a}{4} = \dfrac{x-a}{3}$, then find a in terms of x.

A) $\dfrac{7}{x}$

B) $\dfrac{x}{7}$

C) $7x$

D) $7 - x$

Solution:

$\dfrac{x+a}{4} = \dfrac{x-a}{3}$ (cross multiply)

$4x - 4a = 3x + 3a$

$x = 7a$

$\dfrac{x}{7} = a$

Correct Answer : B

DIGITAL SAT MATH SAMPLE QUESTIONS

Question #13

If $P(x + 1) = 3x + 1$, then what is $P(x + 3)$?

A) $2x + 7$

B) $3x + 7$

C) $-3x + 5$

D) $2x + 1$

Solution:

$P(x + 1) = 3x + 1$

$P((x + 2) + 1) = 3(x + 2) + 1$

$P(x + 3) = 3x + 6 + 1 = 3x + 7$

Correct Answer : B

Question #14

$\dfrac{2x+4}{6} - \dfrac{x}{4} = \dfrac{3}{2}$, find the value of x.

A) 10

B) 12

C) 16

D) 18

Solution:

$\dfrac{2x+4}{6} - \dfrac{x}{4} = \dfrac{3}{2}$

$\dfrac{4x+8}{12} - \dfrac{3x}{12} = \dfrac{18}{12}$ (cancel denominator)

$4x + 8 - 3x = 18$

$x + 8 = 18$

$x = 10$

Correct Answer : A

Question #15

According to the formula $F = \dfrac{9}{5}C + 32°$, the temperature in degrees Fahrenheit for a given temperature in degrees Celsius C. Find the F when $C = 15°$.

A) $15°$

B) $25°$

C) $42°$

D) $59°$

Solution:

$F = \dfrac{9}{5}C + 32°$ since $C = 15°$

$F = \dfrac{9}{5}(15°) + 32°$

$F = 27° + 32°$

$F = 59°$

Correct Answer : D

DIGITAL SAT MATH SAMPLE QUESTIONS

Question #16

If x is a positive integer and $x^2 + x - 20 = 0$, what is the value of $x + 3$?

A) 3

B) 5

C) 7

D) 9

Solution:

$x^2 + x - 20 = 0$

$(x - 4)(x + 5) = 0$

$x - 4 = 0, x = 4$

or

$x + 5 = 0, x = -5$ since x is a positive integer, it cannot be negative.

$x + 3 = 4 + 3 = 7$

Correct Answer : C

Question #17

$i^0 + i^{31} + i^{10}$

Which of the following is equivalent to the complex number shown above? ($i^2 = -1$)

A) i

B) −i

C) 2i

D) −2i

Solution:

Rule: $i^2 = -1$

$= i^0 + i^{31} + i^{10}$

$= 1 + (i^2)^{15} \cdot i + (i^2)^5$

$= 1 + (-1)^{15} \cdot i + (-1)^5$

$= 1 - i - 1$

$= -i$

Correct Answer : B

DIGITAL SAT MATH SAMPLE QUESTIONS

Question #18

$\dfrac{a^{2m}}{a^{10}} = a^{12}$ and $a^{3n} = a^{21}$, then find $m \cdot n$?

A) 55

B) 66

C) 77

D) 88

Solution:

$\dfrac{a^{2m}}{a^{10}} = a^{12}$ and $a^{3n} = a^{21}$.

$a^{2m} = a^{22}$, then $m = 11$.

$a^{3n} = a^{21}$, then $n = 7$

$m \cdot n = 11 \cdot 7 = 77$

Correct Answer : C

Question #19

Write the equation in slope - intercept form for the line that passes through the points $(-2, 4)$ and $(6, -4)$

Solution:

Slope of two points:

$m = \dfrac{y_2 - y_1}{x_2 - x_1}$

$m = \dfrac{-4 - 4}{6 - (-2)} = \dfrac{-8}{8}$

$m = -1$

$y = mx + b$

use $(-2, 4)$ to find b

$y = mx + b$

$4 = -2(-1) + b$

$4 = 2 + b$

$2 = b$

Correct Answer : $y = -x + 2$

REFERENCE SHEET

Directions

For each question from 1 to 17, solve each problem, choose the best answer from the choices provided, and fill in the corresponding bubble on your answer sheet.

For questions 18 to 22, solve the problem and enter your answer in the grid on the answer sheet.

Refer to the directions before question 18 for how to enter your answers in the grid. You may use any available space for scratch work.

REFERENCE

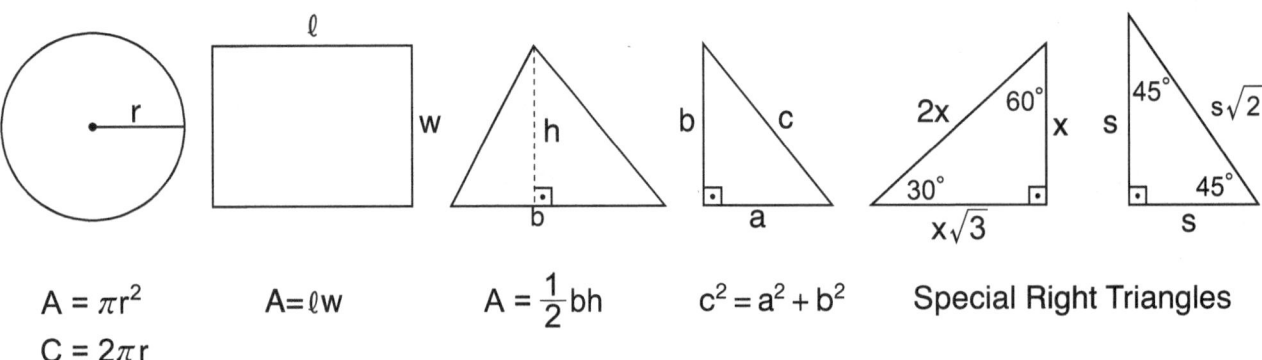

$A = \pi r^2$ $A = \ell w$ $A = \frac{1}{2}bh$ $c^2 = a^2 + b^2$ Special Right Triangles
$C = 2\pi r$

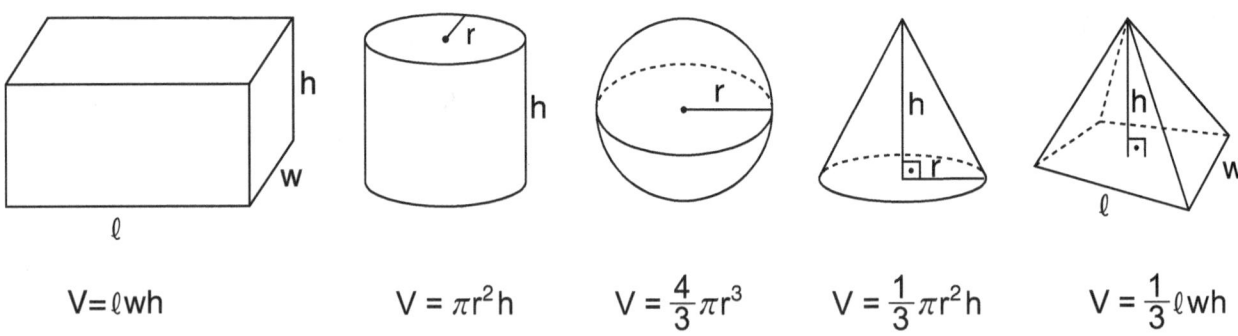

$V = \ell w h$ $V = \pi r^2 h$ $V = \frac{4}{3}\pi r^3$ $V = \frac{1}{3}\pi r^2 h$ $V = \frac{1}{3}\ell w h$

The number of degrees in a circle is 360.

The number of radians in a circle is 2π.

The sum of the measures in degrees of the angles of a triangle is 180.

MATH PRACTICE TEST I
35 Minutes - 22 Questions
MODULE I

1.
$$\begin{cases} \frac{2}{3}x + \frac{3}{4}y = 12 \\ \frac{1}{3}x + \frac{3}{2}y = 18 \end{cases}$$

In the system of equations above, solve for the y value.

A) 3

B) 32

C) $\frac{3}{32}$

D) $\frac{32}{3}$

2.
$$x + 2y = 8$$
$$3x - 2y = 12$$

In the system of equations above, what is the value of x+y?

A) 3

B) 13

C) $\frac{13}{2}$

D) $\frac{2}{13}$

3.
$$(x+3)^2 - 12$$

Which of the following is equivalent to the expression above?

A) $x^2 + 6x - 3$

B) $x^2 + 6x + 3$

C) $x^2 + 3x - 3$

D) $x^2 + 9x + 3$

4.
$$y = mx^2 + 3x + k$$

The graph of the function above has a y-intercept at y = −2 and a x-intercept at x = 2. What is the value of m?

A) 1

B) 0

C) −1

D) −2

5. Melisa is 6 years younger than twice her sister's age. If Melisa is 24 years old, then how old is Melisa's sister?

A) 12

B) 15

C) 17

D) 21

9

MATH PRACTICE TEST I
35 Minutes - 22 Questions
MODULE I

6.
$$f(x) = mx^2 + k$$

In the function above, m and k are constants, $f(0) = 3$, and $f(2) = 7$. What is the value of $f\left(\dfrac{-1}{2}\right)$?

A) 4

B) 13

C) $\dfrac{13}{4}$

D) $\dfrac{4}{13}$

7. If x and y are positive integers and $\sqrt{x} = y^2 = 9$, then which of following is the value of $x - y$?

A) 18

B) 27

C) 48

D) 78

8.

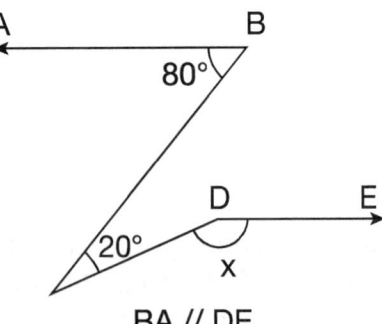

BA // DE

What is the value of x?

A) 70

B) 90

C) 110

D) 120

9.

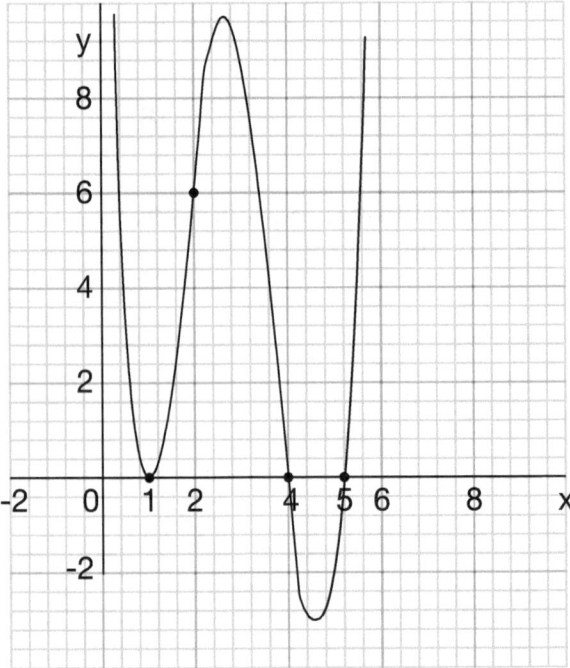

The function $y = f(x)$ is graphed in the xy coordinate plane above. Which of the following equations could describe $f(x)$?

A) $f(x) = (x - 1)^2 \cdot (x - 4) \cdot (x - 5)$

B) $f(x) = (x + 1)^2 \cdot (x - 4) \cdot (x - 5)$

C) $f(x) = (x - 1)^2 \cdot (x + 4) \cdot (x - 5)$

D) $f(x) = (x + 1)^2 \cdot (x + 4) \cdot (x + 5)$

MATH PRACTICE TEST I
35 Minutes - 22 Questions
MODULE I

10. Find the equation of the circle centered at (1, −3) with a radius of 6.

A) $(x - 1)^2 + (y + 3)^2 = 36$

B) $(x - 1)^2 + (y + 3)^2 = 6$

C) $(x + 1)^2 + (y - 3)^2 = 36$

D) $(x + 1)^2 + (y + 3)^2 = 6$

11. $$i^{24} + i^{36} + i^{52}$$

Which of the following is equivalent to the complex number shown above?

A) 1

B) 3

C) i

D) 3i

12. What is the value of g(3) if $g(x) = \dfrac{x^2 - 3x + 5}{x + 1}$?

A) 4

B) 5

C) $\dfrac{4}{5}$

D) $\dfrac{5}{4}$

13. $$\dfrac{x^{\frac{3}{2}} \cdot y^{\frac{3}{5}}}{x^{\frac{1}{2}} \cdot y^{\frac{1}{5}}}$$

Which of the following is equivalent to the expression above, where x and y are positive integers?

A) $x^{\frac{1}{2}} \cdot y^{\frac{3}{5}}$

B) $x^{\frac{1}{2}} \cdot y^{\frac{3}{5}}$

C) $x \cdot y^{\frac{2}{5}}$

D) $x^{\frac{3}{2}} \cdot y^{\frac{3}{5}}$

14. If the expression $\dfrac{1}{5}\left(x + \dfrac{k}{2}\right)\left(x - \dfrac{k}{5}\right)$, where k is a positive constant and can be rewritten as $\dfrac{1}{5}x^2 - 2$, what is the value of k?

A) 5

B) 10

C) 15

D) 25

MATH PRACTICE TEST I
35 Minutes - 22 Questions
MODULE I

15. The total fare of five child movie tickets and one adult movie ticket costs $80. If each child's fare is one–third of each adult's ticket, what is the cost for one child ticket?

A) $10

B) $20

C) $30

D) $40

16.

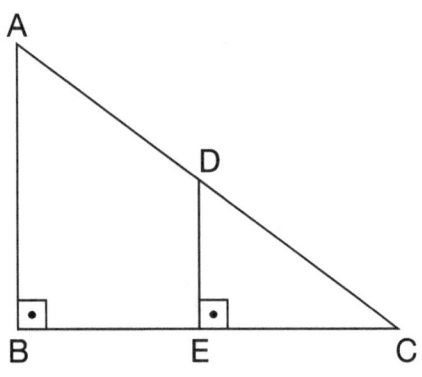

AB // DE

|AB| = 8

|BC| = 6

|DE| = 4, then find |DC| + |EC|?

A) 5

B) 6

C) 7

D) 8

17. If $f(x) = x^2 + 2kx + c$ and the vertex point V is (1, 5), then find $k + c$.

A) 2

B) 4

C) 5

D) 8

18. If $\frac{1}{2}x - \frac{2}{3}y = 20$ and $y = 15$, then find x.

12

MATH PRACTICE TEST I
35 Minutes - 22 Questions
MODULE I

19. If $a = 4\sqrt{3}$ and $5a = \sqrt{20x}$, what is the value of x?

20. If $a - b = 4$ and $a^2 - b^2 = 40$, what is the value of a?

21. In the figure below, O is the center of the circle. If OB = AO = 10cm and BC = 12cm, what is the area of A(ACB)?

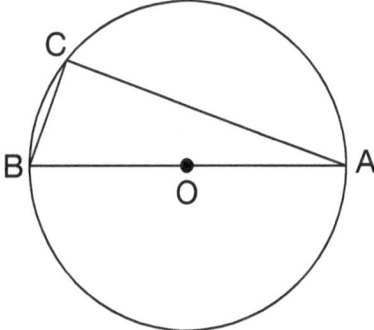

22. If $\frac{1}{2}x - ay - 8 = 0$ and the slope of the equations is $\frac{2}{7}$, then what is the value of a?

PRACTICE TEST I ANSWER SHEET
MODULE I

1. Ⓐ Ⓑ Ⓒ Ⓓ
2. Ⓐ Ⓑ Ⓒ Ⓓ
3. Ⓐ Ⓑ Ⓒ Ⓓ
4. Ⓐ Ⓑ Ⓒ Ⓓ
5. Ⓐ Ⓑ Ⓒ Ⓓ
6. Ⓐ Ⓑ Ⓒ Ⓓ

7. Ⓐ Ⓑ Ⓒ Ⓓ
8. Ⓐ Ⓑ Ⓒ Ⓓ
9. Ⓐ Ⓑ Ⓒ Ⓓ
10. Ⓐ Ⓑ Ⓒ Ⓓ
11. Ⓐ Ⓑ Ⓒ Ⓓ
12. Ⓐ Ⓑ Ⓒ Ⓓ

13. Ⓐ Ⓑ Ⓒ Ⓓ
14. Ⓐ Ⓑ Ⓒ Ⓓ
15. Ⓐ Ⓑ Ⓒ Ⓓ
16. Ⓐ Ⓑ Ⓒ Ⓓ
17. Ⓐ Ⓑ Ⓒ Ⓓ

18.

19.

20.

21.

22.

REFERENCE SHEET

Directions

For each question from 1 to 18, solve each problem, choose the best answer from the choices provided, and fill in the corresponding bubble on your answer sheet.

For questions 19 and 22, solve the problem and enter your answer in the grid on the answer sheet.

Refer to the directions before question 19 for how to enter your answers in the grid. You may use any available space for scratch work.

REFERENCE

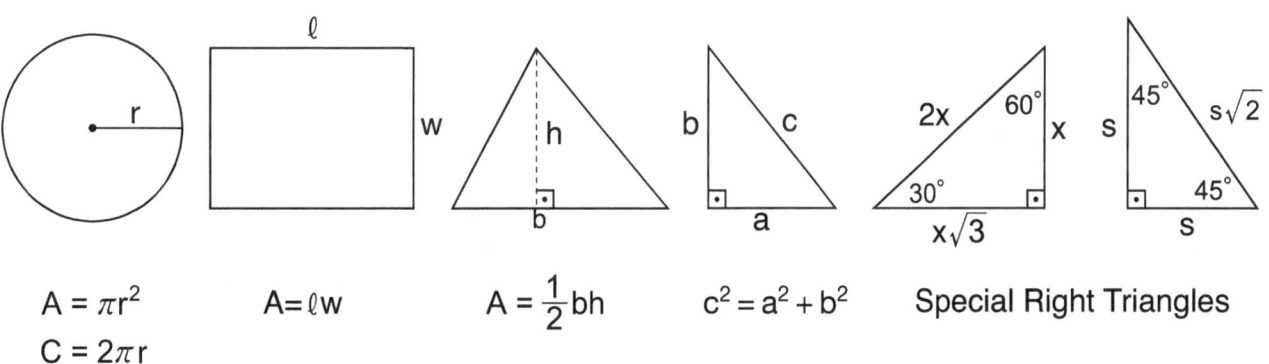

$A = \pi r^2$
$C = 2\pi r$

$A = \ell w$

$A = \dfrac{1}{2} bh$

$c^2 = a^2 + b^2$

Special Right Triangles

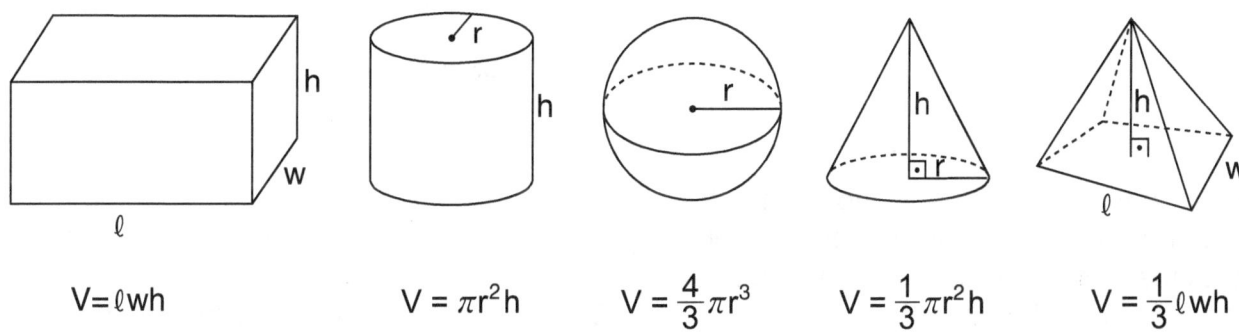

$V = \ell w h$

$V = \pi r^2 h$

$V = \dfrac{4}{3} \pi r^3$

$V = \dfrac{1}{3} \pi r^2 h$

$V = \dfrac{1}{3} \ell w h$

The number of degrees in a circle is 360.

The number of radians in a circle is 2π.

The sum of the measures in degrees of the angles of a triangle is 180.

MATH PRACTICE TEST I
35 Minutes - 22 Questions
MODULE II

1. Which of the following equations passes through the coordinates $(-1, 2)$ and $(3, -6)$?

   A) $y = 2x$

   B) $y = -2x$

   C) $y = 2x + 3$

   D) $y = -2x + 3$

2. $$\frac{\sqrt{yy}}{\sqrt{xx}} - \sqrt{\frac{x}{y}} - \frac{3}{2} = 0$$

   In the above equations, xx and yy are two digit numbers. Which of following could be $x \cdot y$?

   A) 9

   B) 10

   C) 12

   D) 16

3. $$x = \$7 + 11k$$
   $$y = \$15 + 7k$$

   In the equation above, x represents the price in dollars of apple juice and y represents the price in dollars of orange juice at the farmers market. K is the same amount per week. What is the price of orange juice when it's the same as the price of apple juice?

   A) $12

   B) $15

   C) $25

   D) $29

4. On the xy coordinate grid, a line K contains the points $(1, 4)$ and $(-1, 7)$. If the line L is **parallel** to line K at $(3, 1)$, which of following is the equation of the line L?

   A) $y = -\frac{3}{2}x + \frac{11}{2}$

   B) $y = \frac{3}{2}x + \frac{11}{2}$

   C) $y = -\frac{11}{2}x + \frac{3}{2}$

   D) $y = \frac{11}{2}x + \frac{3}{2}$

5. The perimeter of a rectangle is 156cm. If the width of the rectangle is three times the length, what is the width?

   A) 19.5 cm

   B) 31.5 cm

   C) 58.5 cm

   D) 60.5 cm

6. What is the value of x in the equation shown below?

   $$\frac{1}{4}(x-5) + 8 = \frac{1}{2}x + 5$$

   A) 5

   B) 7

   C) 9

   D) 12

16

MATH PRACTICE TEST I
35 Minutes - 22 Questions
MODULE II

7. $\sqrt{a} \cdot \sqrt{a} \cdot \sqrt{a} \cdot \sqrt{a} = 144$. What is the value of a^2?

A) 12

B) 48

C) 144

D) 196

8.
$$\frac{1}{3}x + \frac{1}{4}y = 10$$
$$x - y = 2$$

In the system of equations above, solve for the y value.

A) 12

B) 16

C) 18

D) 20

9. In math team, students are trying to solve an easy test and a hard test. For each correct question in the easy test, students will earn 8 points. For each of the hard test questions, students will earn 18 points. If Jennifer solved a total of 25 questions and earned 300 points in all, how many easy questions did Jennifer solve?

A) 10

B) 15

C) 20

D) 25

10.
$$x - 2ky = 7$$
$$2x + 5y = 15$$

In the system of equations above, k is a constant. For what value of k will the system of equations have no solutions?

A) $\frac{5}{4}$

B) $-\frac{5}{4}$

C) $\frac{1}{2}$

D) $-\frac{1}{2}$

11. x and y are integer numbers.
$$-5 < x < 7$$
$$2 < y < 15$$
What is the maximum value of $x^2 - y^2$?

A) 10

B) 15

C) 20

D) 27

12. If y varies inversely as x and $x = 6$ when $y = 30$, find y when $x = 18$.

A) 5

B) 7

C) 10

D) 12

MATH PRACTICE TEST I
35 Minutes - 22 Questions
MODULE II

13. If a, b, and c are positive numbers and $a \cdot b = \frac{1}{2}$, $b \cdot c = \frac{1}{4}$ and $a \cdot c = \frac{1}{8}$, then find $a \cdot b \cdot c$?

A) $\frac{1}{2}$

B) $\frac{1}{4}$

C) $\frac{1}{6}$

D) $\frac{1}{8}$

14. If $P(x-2) = x^2 + 2x + 1$, then find $P(x+1)$?

A) $x^2 + 8x + 16$

B) $-x^2 + 8x + 16$

C) $x^2 - 8x + 16$

D) $x^2 + 8x - 16$

15. There are 48 students in Science class and they are completing their classwork and then turn to their group to discuss their work. The ratio of complete work to incomplete work was 5 to 7. How many students did not complete their classwork?

A) 20

B) 22

C) 28

D) 32

16.
$$-3 < p < 2$$
$$2 < q < 5$$

From the above inequality, what is the biggest value of $p^2 + 2q$?

A) 15

B) 16

C) 17

D) 18

17. In the following figure, what is the measure of a?

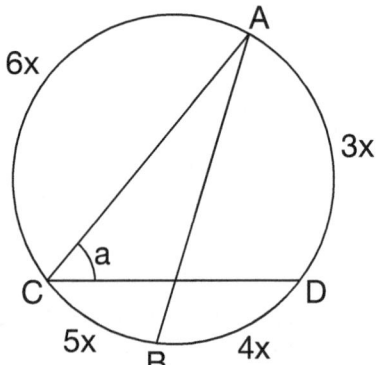

A) 15°

B) 25°

C) 30°

D) 45°

MATH PRACTICE TEST I
35 Minutes - 22 Questions
MODULE II

18. $A = 3x+1 = 4y+2 = 5z+3$

From the above equations x, y, and z are positive integer and A is a two digit number. What is the smallest value of A?

A) 58

B) 88

C) 108

D) 128

19. The population of Town A is 1.2×10^6 and the population of Town B is 24×10^3. How many times the population of Town A is greater than population of Town B?

20.

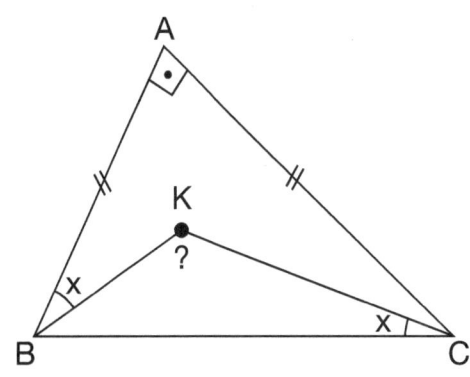

Find the angle of $\angle (BKC)$.

21. If a and b are positive integers when $a^2 - 3b = 28$ and $b = 7$, then find a.

22. If $3x - 2y = 4$, then find $\dfrac{8^x}{4^y}$.

PRACTICE TEST I ANSWER SHEET
MODULE II

1. Ⓐ Ⓑ Ⓒ Ⓓ
2. Ⓐ Ⓑ Ⓒ Ⓓ
3. Ⓐ Ⓑ Ⓒ Ⓓ
4. Ⓐ Ⓑ Ⓒ Ⓓ
5. Ⓐ Ⓑ Ⓒ Ⓓ
6. Ⓐ Ⓑ Ⓒ Ⓓ

7. Ⓐ Ⓑ Ⓒ Ⓓ
8. Ⓐ Ⓑ Ⓒ Ⓓ
9. Ⓐ Ⓑ Ⓒ Ⓓ
10. Ⓐ Ⓑ Ⓒ Ⓓ
11. Ⓐ Ⓑ Ⓒ Ⓓ
12. Ⓐ Ⓑ Ⓒ Ⓓ

13. Ⓐ Ⓑ Ⓒ Ⓓ
14. Ⓐ Ⓑ Ⓒ Ⓓ
15. Ⓐ Ⓑ Ⓒ Ⓓ
16. Ⓐ Ⓑ Ⓒ Ⓓ
17. Ⓐ Ⓑ Ⓒ Ⓓ
18. Ⓐ Ⓑ Ⓒ Ⓓ

19.
20.
21.
22.

PRACTICE TEST I
MODULE I ANSWER KEY

1)	D
2)	C
3)	A
4)	C
5)	B
6)	C
7)	D
8)	D
9)	A
10)	A
11)	B
12)	D
13)	C
14)	B
15)	A
16)	D
17)	C
18)	60
19)	60
20)	7
21)	96 cm
22)	7/4

PRACTICE TEST I
MODULE I SOLUTIONS

1. $\left.\begin{array}{l}\frac{2}{3}x+\frac{3}{4}y=12\\-2\cdot\left(\frac{1}{3}x+\frac{3}{2}y=18\right)\end{array}\right]$ $\begin{array}{l}\frac{2}{3}x+\frac{3}{4}y=12\\-\frac{2}{3}x-3y=-36\end{array}$

$\frac{3}{4}y-3y=-24$

$\frac{-9y}{4}=-24$

$\frac{9y}{4}=24$, $y=\frac{4\cdot 24}{9}$

$y=\frac{32}{3}$

Correct Answer : D

2. $\begin{array}{r}x+2y=8\\3x-2y=12\\\hline\end{array}$ +

$4x=20$

$x=5$

$x+2y=8$

$5+2y=8$

$2y=8-5$

$2y=3$

$y=\frac{3}{2}$

$x+y=5+\frac{3}{2}=\frac{13}{2}$

Correct Answer : C

3. $(x+3)^2-12=(x+3)\cdot(x+3)-12$

$=x^2+3x+3x+9-12$

$=x^2+6x-3$

Correct Answer : A

4. $y=mx^2+3x+k$

y – intercept at $y=-2$, $x=0$

$-2=m\cdot 0^2+3\cdot 0+k$

$-2=k$

x – intercept at $x=2$, $y=0$

$0=m\cdot 2^2+3\cdot 2+k$

$0=4m+6+k$

$0=4m+6-2$

$0=4m+4$

$-4=4m$

$-1=m$

Correct Answer : C

5. $\underline{\text{Melisa}}\quad\underline{\text{Her sister}}$
$\;\;2x-6\qquad\quad x$

$2x-6=24$

$2x=30$

$x=15$

Correct Answer : B

PRACTICE TEST I
MODULE I SOLUTIONS

6. $f(x) = mx^2 + k$

$f(0) = 3$

$f(0) = m \cdot 0^2 + k$

$3 = 0 + k$

$3 = k$

$f(x) = mx^2 + 3$

$f(2) = m \cdot 2^2 + 3$

$7 = 4m + 3$

$4 = 4m$

$1 = m$

$f(x) = x^2 + 3$

$f\left(-\frac{1}{2}\right) = \left(-\frac{1}{2}\right)^2 + 3$

$= \frac{1}{4} + 3$

$= \frac{13}{4}$

Correct Answer : C

8.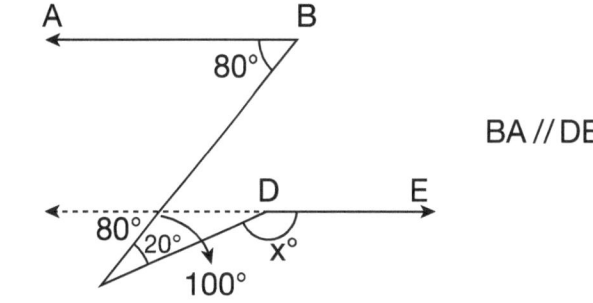

BA // DE

$x° = 100° + 20°$

$x = 120°$

Correct Answer : D

9. Since the graph has x − intercept at x = 1, x = 4 and x = 5, then by the Factor They are the polynomid must have factors of (x − 1) . (x − 4) . (x − 5)

Also, the graph contains the point (2, 6).

This point satisfies the function in choice A.

Correct Answer : A

7. $\sqrt{x} = 9$, $x = 81$
$y^2 = 9$, $y = 3$ $\Big\}$ $x - y = 81 - 3 = 78$

Correct Answer : D

10. $(x - h)^2 + (y - k)^2 = r^2$

$(x - 1)^2 + (y + 3)^2 = 36$

Correct Answer : A

23

PRACTICE TEST I
MODULE I SOLUTIONS

11. $i^{24} + i^{36} + i^{52}$

$\boxed{\text{Rule: } i^2 = -1}$

$= (i^2)^{12} + (i^2)^{18} + (i^2)^{26}$

$= (-1)^{12} + (-1)^{18} + (-1)^{26}$

$= 1 + 1 + 1$

$= 3$

Correct Answer : B

12. $g(x) = \dfrac{x^2 - 3x + 5}{x + 1}$

$g(3) = \dfrac{3^2 - 3 \cdot 3 + 5}{3 + 1}$

$= \dfrac{9 - 9 + 5}{4}$

$= \dfrac{5}{4}$

Correct Answer : D

13. $\dfrac{x^{\frac{3}{2}} \cdot y^{\frac{3}{5}}}{x^{\frac{1}{2}} \cdot x^{\frac{1}{5}}} = x^{\frac{3}{2} - \frac{1}{2}} \cdot y^{\frac{3}{5} - \frac{1}{5}}$

$= x^{\frac{2}{2}} \cdot y^{\frac{2}{5}}$

$= x \cdot y^{\frac{2}{5}}$

Correct Answer : C

14. $\dfrac{1}{5}\left(x + \dfrac{k}{2}\right) \cdot \left(x - \dfrac{k}{5}\right) = \dfrac{1}{5}x^2 - 2$

$\dfrac{1}{5}\left(x^2 - \dfrac{k^2}{10}\right) = \dfrac{1}{5}x^2 - 2$

$\dfrac{1}{5}x^2 - \dfrac{k^2}{50} = \dfrac{1}{5}x^2 - 2$

$\dfrac{-k^2}{50} = -2$

$k^2 = 100$, $k = \mp 10$

$k = 10$ (since k is positive integers)

Correct Answer : B

15. Child ticket + Adult ticket = Total Fare

$5C + A = \$80$

If each child's ticket is $\dfrac{1}{3}$ of adult ticket

$C = \dfrac{1}{3}A$, $A = 3C$

$5C + A = \$80$

$5C + 3C = \$80$ $8C = \$80$

$C = \$10$

Correct Answer : A

PRACTICE TEST I
MODULE I SOLUTIONS

16.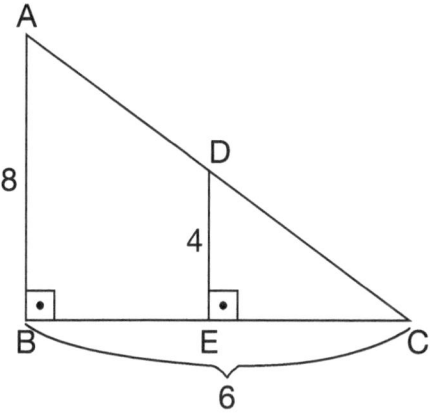

$|AC| = 6^2 + 8^2 = 10^2$

$|AC| = 10$

$\dfrac{4}{8} = \dfrac{|DC|}{|AC|}$, $\dfrac{1}{2} = \dfrac{|DC|}{10}$

$|DC| = 5$

$\dfrac{1}{2} = \dfrac{|EC|}{|BC|}$, $\dfrac{1}{2} = \dfrac{|EC|}{6}$

$|EC| = 3$

$|DC| + |EC| = 5 + 3 = 8$

Correct Answer : D

17. $f(x) = x^2 + 2kx + c$

$x = \dfrac{-b}{2a}$ (Axis of symmetry)

$x = \dfrac{-b}{2a}$

$x = \dfrac{-2k}{2}$

$1 = \dfrac{-2k}{2}$ (since x = 1)

$2 = -2k$

$-1 = k$

V(1, 5) → plug this point in to the equation

$5 = 1^2 + 2k(1) + c$

$4 = 2k + c$, $k = -1$

$4 = 2(-1) + c$

$4 + 2 = c$

$6 = c$

$k + c = 6 + (-1) = 5$

Correct Answer : C

25

PRACTICE TEST I
MODULE I SOLUTIONS

18. $\frac{1}{2}x - \frac{2}{3}y = 20$, $y = 15$

$\frac{1}{2}x - \frac{2}{3}(15) = 20$

$\frac{1}{2}x - \frac{30}{3} = 20$

$\frac{1}{2}x - 10 = 20$

$\frac{1}{2}x = 30$

$x = 60$

Correct Answer : 60

19. $a = 4\sqrt{3}$ and $5a = \sqrt{20x}$

$5(4\sqrt{3}) = \sqrt{20x}$

$(20\sqrt{3})^2 = (\sqrt{20x})^2$

$400 \cdot 3 = 20x$

$\frac{1200}{20} = x$

$60 = x$

Correct Answer : 60

20. $a - b = 4$ and $a^2 - b^2 = 40$

$(a - b) \cdot (a + b) = 40$

$4(a + b) = 40$

$a + b = 10$

$a - b = 4$
$\underline{+\ a + b = 10}$
$2a = 14 \quad a = 7$

Correct Answer : 7

21.

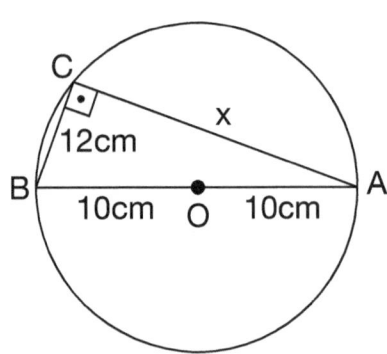

Use pythagorean theorem for right triangle.

$(12cm)^2 + x^2 = (20cm)^2$

$144cm^2 + x^2 = 400cm^2$

$x^2 = 400cm^2 - 144cm^2$

$x^2 = 256cm^2$

$x = 16cm$

Area of A(ACB) $= \frac{12cm \cdot 16cm}{2} = 96cm^2$

Correct Answer : 96cm²

22. $\frac{1}{2}x - ay = 8$

slope intercept form $\quad y = mx + b$

$\frac{1}{2}x - 8 = ay$

$\frac{1}{2a}x - \frac{8}{a} = y \quad$ slope $= \frac{1}{2a}$

$\frac{1}{2a} = \frac{2}{7}$, $4a = 7$

$a = \frac{7}{4}$

Correct Answer : $\frac{7}{4}$

PRACTICE TEST I
MODULE II ANSWER KEY

1)	B
2)	D
3)	D
4)	A
5)	C
6)	B
7)	C
8)	B
9)	B
10)	B
11)	D

12)	C
13)	D
14)	A
15)	C
16)	D
17)	C
18)	A
19)	50
20)	135°
21)	7
22)	16

PRACTICE TEST I
MODULE II SOLUTIONS

1. The slope of points $(-1, -2)$ and $(3, -6)$.

$m = \dfrac{y_2 - y_1}{x_2 - x_1}$

$m = \dfrac{-6 - (2)}{3 - (-1)} = \dfrac{-8}{4} = -2$

Slope - intercept form

$y = mx + b$

$y = -2x + b$, (use one of the above points to find b constant)

$-6 = -2(3) + b$

$-6 = -6 + b$

$-6 + 6 = b$

$0 = b$

$y = -2x$

Correct Answer : B

2. $\sqrt{\dfrac{11y}{11x}} - \sqrt{\dfrac{x}{y}} - \dfrac{3}{2} = 0$

$\dfrac{\sqrt{y}}{\sqrt{x}} - \dfrac{\sqrt{x}}{\sqrt{y}} = \dfrac{3}{2}$ (Find common denominator)

$\dfrac{\sqrt{y} \cdot (\sqrt{y})}{\sqrt{x} \cdot (\sqrt{y})} - \dfrac{\sqrt{x} \cdot (\sqrt{x})}{\sqrt{y} \cdot (\sqrt{x})} = \dfrac{3}{2}$

$\dfrac{\sqrt{y^2}}{\sqrt{xy}} - \dfrac{\sqrt{x^2}}{\sqrt{xy}} = \dfrac{3}{2}$

$\dfrac{y}{\sqrt{xy}} - \dfrac{x}{\sqrt{xy}} = \dfrac{3}{2}$

$\dfrac{y - x}{\sqrt{xy}} = \dfrac{3}{2}$, then x could be 8 and y could be 2.

$x \cdot y = 2 \cdot 8 = 16$

Correct Answer : D

3. $x = \$7 + 11k \longrightarrow$ price of apple juice

$y = \$15 + 7k \longrightarrow$ price of orange juice

$x = y$ because price of orange juice is the same as the price of apple juice.

$\$7 + 11k = \$15 + 7k$

$11k - 7k = \$15 - \$7$

$4k = \$8$

$k = \$2$

$y = \$15 + 7k \longrightarrow$ price of orange juice

$y = \$15 + 7(\$2)$

$y = \$15 + \$14$

$y = \$29$

Correct Answer : D

4. Line K contains the points $(1, 4)$ and $(-1, 7)$.

Slope of point K

$m = \dfrac{y_2 - y_1}{x_2 - x_1} = \dfrac{7 - 4}{-1 - (1)} = \dfrac{3}{-2} = -\dfrac{3}{2}$

Since line K is parallel to line L slopes are same.

Slope of point L is $-\dfrac{3}{2}$.

Slope - intercept form

$y = mx + b$

$y = -\dfrac{3}{2}x + b$ (use one of the above points to find b constant)

$7 = -\dfrac{3}{2}(-1) + b$

$7 = \dfrac{3}{2} + b$

$7 - \dfrac{3}{2} = b$

$\dfrac{11}{2} = b$

Equation of line L $\longrightarrow y = -\dfrac{3}{2} + \dfrac{11}{2}$

Correct Answer : A

PRACTICE TEST I
MODULE II SOLUTIONS

5. The perimeter of the rectangular is 156cm.

2L + 2W = 156cm

W = 3L

2L + 2(3L) = 156cm

2L + 6L = 156cm

8L = 156cm

L = 19.5cm

W = 58.5cm

Correct Answer : C

6. $\frac{1}{4}(x-5)+8=\frac{1}{2}x+5$

$4 \cdot \left[\frac{1}{4}(x-5)+8=\frac{1}{2}x+5\right]$

(Multiply both sides of the equation of equation with common factors to take out denominators)

$\frac{4x}{4}-\frac{20}{4}+32=\frac{4x}{2}+20$

x − 5 + 32 = 2x + 20

x + 27 = 2x + 20

27 − 20 = 2x − x , x = 7

Correct Answer : B

7. $\frac{\sqrt{a}\cdot\sqrt{a}}{a}\cdot\frac{\sqrt{a}\cdot\sqrt{a}}{a}=144$

$a^2 = 144$

Correct Answer : C

8. $\frac{1}{3}x+\frac{1}{4}y=10$

(Multiply both side of equation with common factors to take out denominators)

$12\left[\frac{1}{3}x+\frac{1}{4}y=10\right]=4x+3y=120$

$\begin{pmatrix}4x+3y=120\\3(x-y=2)\end{pmatrix}$ Use elimination method to find x and y.

(4x + 3y = 120)

+ (3x − 3y = 6)
_____

7x = 126

x = 18

y = 16

Correct Answer : B

9. Easy questions: e

Hard questions: h

$\begin{pmatrix}e+h=25\\8e+18h=2\end{pmatrix}$ Use elimination method to find e and h.

$\begin{pmatrix}-8(e+h=25)\\8e+18h=300\end{pmatrix}=\begin{pmatrix}-8e-8h=-200\\8e+18h=300\end{pmatrix}$

10h = 100, then h = 10 and e = 15.

Correct Answer : B

PRACTICE TEST I
MODULE II SOLUTIONS

10. If the systems of equations have no solutions that mean equations have same slope.

$$x - 2ky = 7$$
$$2x + 5y = 15$$

NOTE: slope is a number next to the x–axis over a number next to the y–axis and sing is always opposite.

Slope of 1st equation is : $\dfrac{1}{2k}$

Slope of 2nd equation is : $-\dfrac{2}{5}$

Since slopes are equal.

$$\dfrac{1}{2k} = -\dfrac{2}{5}$$

$$-4k = 5$$

$$k = -\dfrac{5}{4}$$

Correct Answer : B

11. $-5 < x < 7$
$2 < y < 15$

since x and y are integers, x maximum can be 6 and y minimum can be 3.

$$x^2 - y^2 = 6^2 - 3^2$$
$$= 36 - 9$$
$$= 27$$

Correct Answer : D

12. $y = \dfrac{k}{x}$ (inverse variation)

If x = 6 when y = 30, then $30 = \dfrac{k}{6}$ and k = 180.

Use the same formula to find y when x = 18.

$$y = \dfrac{k}{x} \longrightarrow y = \dfrac{180}{18}, \text{ then } y=10$$

Correct Answer : C

13. $a \cdot b = \dfrac{1}{2}$

$b \cdot c = \dfrac{1}{4}$

$a \cdot c = \dfrac{1}{8}$

Let multiply all together;

$$a^2 \cdot b^2 \cdot c^2 = \dfrac{1}{2} \cdot \dfrac{1}{4} \cdot \dfrac{1}{8}$$

$$a^2 \cdot b^2 \cdot c^2 = \dfrac{1}{64}$$

$$\sqrt{a^2 \cdot b^2 \cdot c^2} = \sqrt{\dfrac{1}{64}}$$

$a \cdot b \cdot c = \pm \dfrac{1}{8}$, Since a, b, and c are positive numbers

$a \cdot b \cdot c = \dfrac{1}{8}$

Correct Answer : D

14. $P(x - 2) = x^2 + 2x + 1$

To find P (x + 1) plug in x + 3 for x in P(x – 2).

$$P(x + 3 - 2) = (x + 3)^2 + 2(x + 3) + 1$$

$$P(x + 1) = x^2 + 6x + 9 + 2x + 6 + 1$$

$$P(x + 1) = x^2 + 8x + 16$$

Correct Answer : A

PRACTICE TEST I
MODULE II SOLUTIONS

15. Ratio of complete work to incomplete work is 5 to 7.

$5x + 7x = 48$

$12x = 48$

$x = 4$

Complete work: $5x = 5 \cdot 4 = 20$

Incomplete work: $7x = 7 \cdot 4 = 28$

Correct Answer : C

17.

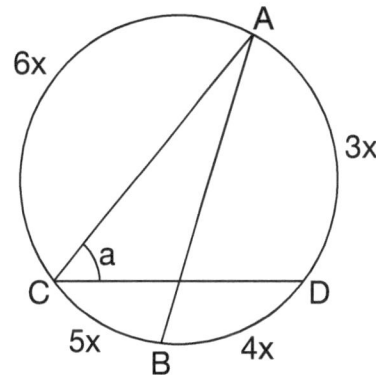

$6x + 5x + 4x + 3x = 360°$

$18x = 360°$

$x = 20$, $2a = 3x$

$2a = 60°$, $a = 30°$

Correct Answer : C

16. $p^2 \longrightarrow 4 < p^2 < 9$

$2q \longrightarrow 4 < 2q < 10$

$\underline{\quad + \quad\quad\quad\quad\quad\quad}$

$8 < p^2 + 2q < 19$

Highest value of $p^2 + 2q$ is 18.

Correct Answer : D

18. If $A = 3x + 1 = 4y + 2 = 5z + 3$,

then $A + 2 = 3x + 3 = 4y + 4 = 5z + 5$.

$A + 2 = 3(x + 1) = 4(y + 1) = 5(z + 1)$

$A + 2 = $ LCM $(3, 4, 5) = 60$.

$A + 2 = 60$,   then $A = 58$

Correct Answer : A

PRACTICE TEST I
MODULE II SOLUTIONS

19. Town A is 1.2×10^6

Town B is 24×10^3

$\dfrac{\text{population of Town A}}{\text{population of Town B}} = \dfrac{1.2 \times 10^6}{24 \times 10^3}$

$\dfrac{12 \times 10^5}{24 \times 10^3} = \dfrac{1 \times 10^5}{2 \times 10^3} = \dfrac{1}{2} \cdot 10^{5-3}$

$= \dfrac{1}{2} \cdot 10^2$

$= 50$

Correct Answer : 50

21. $a^2 - 3b = 28$ and $b = 7$

$a^2 - 3(7) = 28$

$a^2 - 21 = 28$

$a^2 = 28 + 21$

$a^2 = 49$

$a = \pm 7$ (since a is positive integer a can be only 7)

$a = 7$

Correct Answer : 7

20.

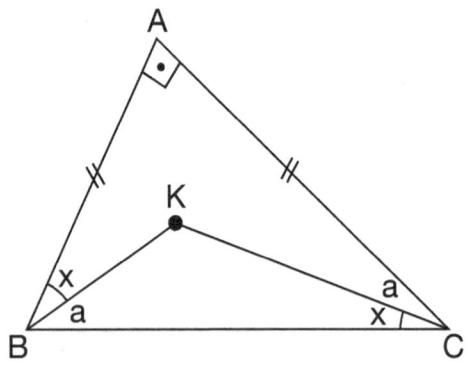

$2x + 2a + 90° = 180°$

$x + a = 45°$

$\angle(BCK) + x + a = 180°$

$\angle(BCK) + 45° = 180°$

$\angle(BCK) = 135°$

Correct Answer : 135°

22. $3x - 3y = 4$

$\dfrac{8^x}{4^y} = \dfrac{2^{3x}}{2^{2y}} = 2^{3x-2y} = 2^4 = 16$

Correct Answer : 16

32

REFERENCE SHEET

Directions

For each question from 1 to 17, solve each problem, choose the best answer from the choices provided, and fill in the corresponding bubble on your answer sheet.

For questions 18 to 22, solve the problem and enter your answer in the grid on the answer sheet.

Refer to the directions before question 18 for how to enter your answers in the grid. You may use any available space for scratch work.

REFERENCE

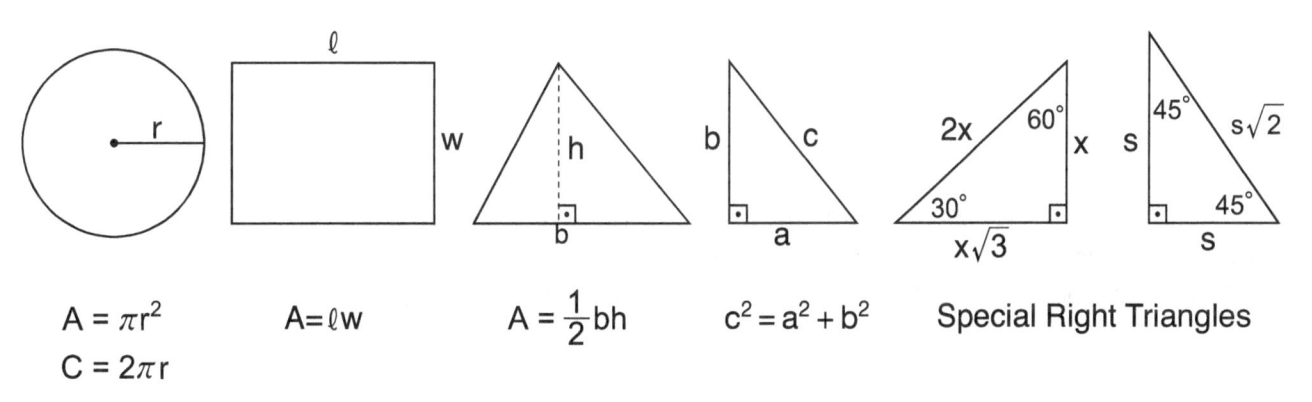

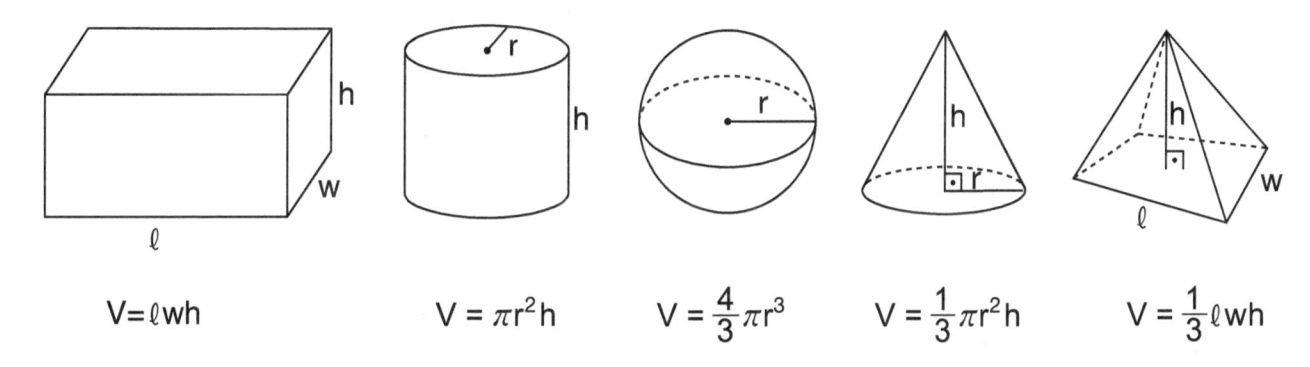

$A = \pi r^2$
$C = 2\pi r$

$A = \ell w$

$A = \frac{1}{2}bh$

$c^2 = a^2 + b^2$

Special Right Triangles

$V = \ell w h$

$V = \pi r^2 h$

$V = \frac{4}{3}\pi r^3$

$V = \frac{1}{3}\pi r^2 h$

$V = \frac{1}{3}\ell w h$

The number of degrees in a circle is 360.

The number of radians in a circle is 2π.

The sum of the measures in degrees of the angles of a triangle is 180.

MATH PRACTICE TEST II
35 Minutes - 22 Questions
MODULE I

1. Which of the following is equivalent to $\left(x+\dfrac{x}{2}\right)^2$?

   A) $\dfrac{x^2}{4}$

   B) $\dfrac{9x^2}{4}$

   C) $\dfrac{4x^2}{9}$

   D) $\dfrac{5x^2}{4}$

2. The height of a trunk is between $\sqrt{2}$ meters and $\sqrt{8}$ meters. Which of the following could be the height of the trunk?

   A) $\dfrac{1}{65}$

   B) $\dfrac{5}{2}$

   C) $\dfrac{37}{8}$

   D) $\dfrac{11}{3}$

3. How many liters of 80% pure water must be added to 40 liters of a 30% pure water to produce 60% pure water?

   A) 30 liters

   B) 40 liters

   C) 50 liters

   D) 60 liters

4. $$2a + 3b = 18$$
   $$3b - 5a = 11$$
   What is the value of a − b?

   A) 3

   B) 13

   C) $\dfrac{-13}{3}$

   D) $\dfrac{13}{3}$

5. The population of a city is increased from 120,000 to 168,000. Find the percentage of the increase.

   A) 20%

   B) 30%

   C) 40%

   D) 50%

6. What is the solution to the equation below?

   $$\dfrac{2}{x-3} = \dfrac{5}{2x-7}$$

   A) 1

   B) −1

   C) 2

   D) −2

MATH PRACTICE TEST II
35 Minutes - 22 Questions
MODULE I

7. If $x^3 = 64$, then find x^2.

A) 2

B) 4

C) 8

D) 16

8. Henry went to the supermarket. He needed to buy 8 eggs and 4 liter of milk. 1 egg cost $2 and 1 liter of milk cost 2^2. At the end of shopping trip he paid 2^a. Find the value of a.

A) 3

B) 4

C) 5

D) 6

9. What is the solution of the equation given below?

$$\frac{\sqrt{2} \cdot 6^{\frac{1}{3}}}{\sqrt[3]{3} \cdot 2^{-\frac{1}{6}}}$$

A) 1

B) 2

C) 3

D) 4

10. Tom has a garden, which is 24 feet in height and 32 feet in width. He wants to plant trees around his garden. The price of a tree is $5. At least how much does he have to pay for the trees?

A) $50

B) $60

C) $70

D) $80

11. The sum of the three consecutive even numbers is 42. What is half of the smallest number?

A) 4

B) 6

C) 8

D) 10

MATH PRACTICE TEST II
35 Minutes - 22 Questions
MODULE I

12.

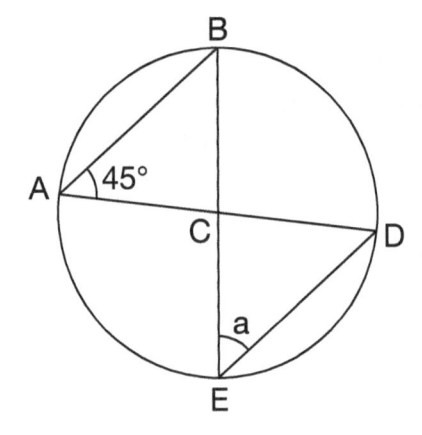

If C is the center of the circle then find the a.

A) 40°

B) 45°

C) 100°

D) 120°

13. Which of the following is equal to $\frac{x^2}{9} - \frac{y^2}{4}$?

A) $\left(\frac{x}{3} - \frac{y}{2}\right) \cdot \left(\frac{x}{3} - \frac{y}{2}\right)$

B) $\left(\frac{x}{3} + \frac{y}{2}\right) \cdot \left(\frac{x}{3} - \frac{y}{2}\right)$

C) $\left(\frac{x}{3} + \frac{y}{2}\right) \cdot \left(\frac{x}{3} + \frac{y}{2}\right)$

D) $\left(\frac{x}{2} - \frac{y}{3}\right) \cdot \left(\frac{x}{2} + \frac{y}{3}\right)$

14. $\frac{3(x+5) - 8}{7} = \frac{17 - (6-x)}{5}$

In the equation above, what is the value of x?

A) $\frac{21}{4}$

B) $\frac{11}{4}$

C) $\frac{4}{21}$

D) $\frac{23}{4}$

15. Which of the following complex numbers are equivalent to $\left(\frac{1+i}{1-i}\right)^{2018}$?

A) 1

B) −1

C) i

D) −i

MATH PRACTICE TEST II
35 Minutes - 22 Questions
MODULE I

16.

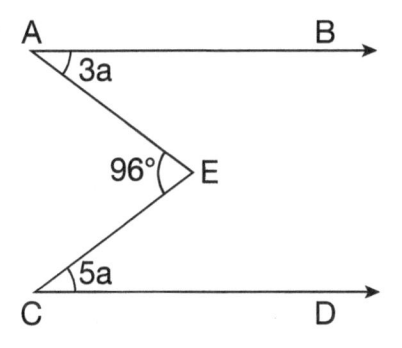

In the figure above, AB is parallel to CD. What is the angle of $\angle(BAE)$?

17. What is the sum of the solutions for $x^2 + x - 12 = 0$?

A) -2

B) -1

C) 1

D) 2

18.
$$2a - 3b = 12$$
$$3a + 5b = 18$$

For the solution (a, b) to the system of equations above, what is the value of $a - b$?

A) 2

B) 4

C) 6

D) 8

19. What is the average test score for the class if 6 students received scores of: 88, 85, 95, 66, 75 and 80?

20. In the polynomial below c is the constant. If the polynomial f(x) is divisible by x−4 then find the value of c.

$$f(x) = x^2 - 2cx + 8$$

21. If $x = 1 - \sqrt{3}$ and $y = 1 + \sqrt{3}$ then find $x \cdot y$?

22. If $x^2 + ax - 10 = (x - 1)(bx + c)$ then find $a + c$.

PRACTICE TEST II ANSWER SHEET
MODULE I

1. Ⓐ Ⓑ Ⓒ Ⓓ
2. Ⓐ Ⓑ Ⓒ Ⓓ
3. Ⓐ Ⓑ Ⓒ Ⓓ
4. Ⓐ Ⓑ Ⓒ Ⓓ
5. Ⓐ Ⓑ Ⓒ Ⓓ
6. Ⓐ Ⓑ Ⓒ Ⓓ

7. Ⓐ Ⓑ Ⓒ Ⓓ
8. Ⓐ Ⓑ Ⓒ Ⓓ
9. Ⓐ Ⓑ Ⓒ Ⓓ
10. Ⓐ Ⓑ Ⓒ Ⓓ
11. Ⓐ Ⓑ Ⓒ Ⓓ
12. Ⓐ Ⓑ Ⓒ Ⓓ

13. Ⓐ Ⓑ Ⓒ Ⓓ
14. Ⓐ Ⓑ Ⓒ Ⓓ
15. Ⓐ Ⓑ Ⓒ Ⓓ
16. Ⓐ Ⓑ Ⓒ Ⓓ
17. Ⓐ Ⓑ Ⓒ Ⓓ
18. Ⓐ Ⓑ Ⓒ Ⓓ

REFERENCE SHEET

Directions

For each question from 1 to 18, solve each problem, choose the best answer from the choices provided, and fill in the corresponding bubble on your answer sheet.

For questions 18 and 22, solve the problem and enter your answer in the grid on the answer sheet.

Refer to the directions before question 18 for how to enter your answers in the grid. You may use any available space for scratch work.

REFERENCE

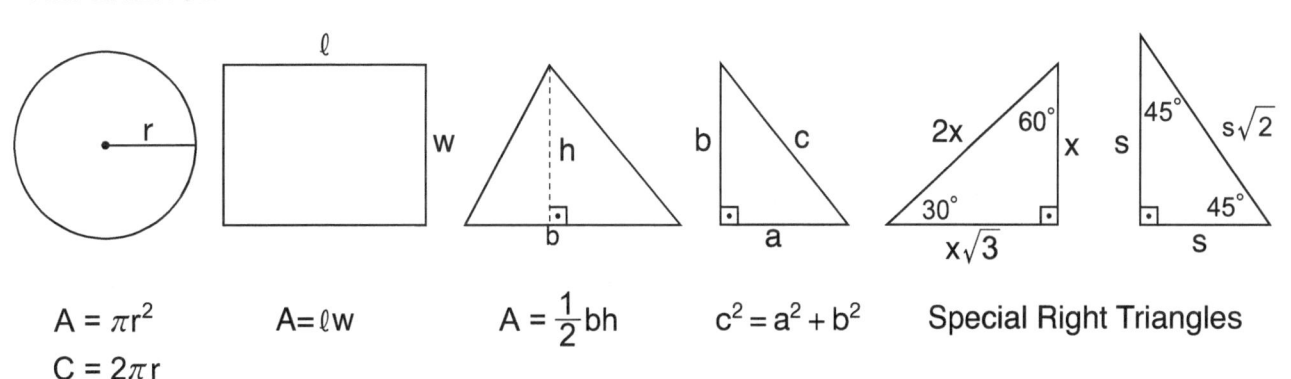

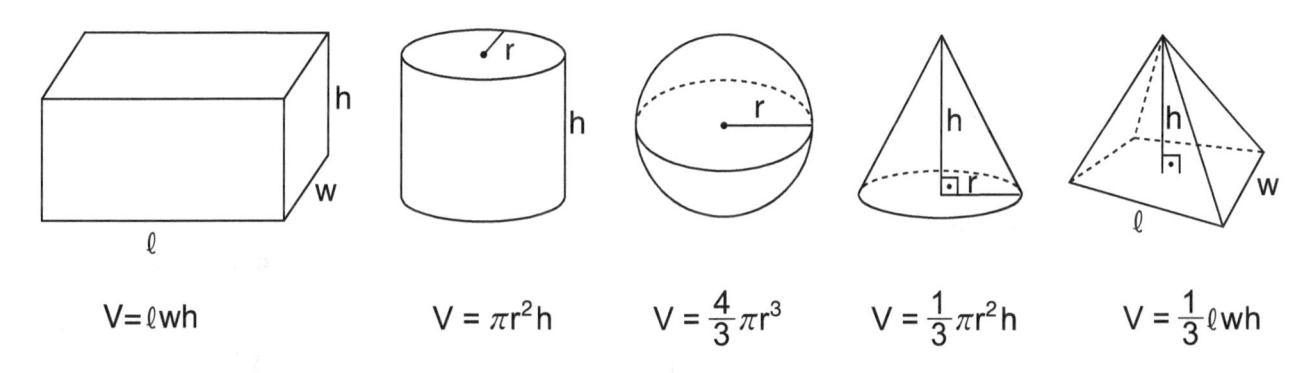

$A = \pi r^2$
$C = 2\pi r$

$A = \ell w$

$A = \frac{1}{2}bh$

$c^2 = a^2 + b^2$

Special Right Triangles

$V = \ell w h$

$V = \pi r^2 h$

$V = \frac{4}{3}\pi r^3$

$V = \frac{1}{3}\pi r^2 h$

$V = \frac{1}{3}\ell w h$

The number of degrees in a circle is 360.

The number of radians in a circle is 2π.

The sum of the measures in degrees of the angles of a triangle is 180.

MATH PRACTICE TEST II
35 Minutes - 22 Questions
MODULE II

1. What is the solution of the equation given below?

   $$\frac{\sqrt{3} \cdot \sqrt[3]{27}}{\sqrt[3]{8} \cdot \sqrt{2}}?$$

   A) $\frac{3\sqrt{2}}{4}$

   B) $\frac{2\sqrt{2}}{3}$

   C) $\sqrt{2}$

   D) $\sqrt{3}$

2. Let A and B be two sets.
   A = {−7, −6, −5, −4, −3, −2, −1, 0, 1, 2, 3, 4, 5, 6}
   B = {−9, −7, −5, −3, −1, 3, 5, 7, 9}
   Which of the following is the given set of s(A ∩ B)?

   A) (−9, −5, −3, −1, 0, 1, 3, 5)

   B) (−7, −5, −3, −1, 3, 5)

   C) (−9, −7, −5, −3, −1, 3, 5, 6)

   D) (−7, −5, −3, −1, 1, 2, 3, 4, 5)

3. In a college there will be an election for the head of students. There are three candidates: Mike, Julia, and Peter. Mike has 30% of the votes, Julia has 60% of votes, and Peter has 10% of votes. In the election 500 votes were collected. What is difference between Julia and Mike?

   A) 50

   B) 150

   C) 200

   D) 250

4. $f(x) = 3x - 6$. What is the solution of $f(2) + f^{-1}(3)$?

   A) 1

   B) 2

   C) 3

   D) 4

5. A{0, 1, 2, 3, 4, 5, 6, 7, 8, 9}

   What is the probability of the selecting an odd number in the set A?

   A) $\frac{1}{2}$

   B) $\frac{1}{3}$

   C) $\frac{1}{4}$

   D) $\frac{1}{5}$

MATH PRACTICE TEST II
35 Minutes - 22 Questions
MODULE II

6.

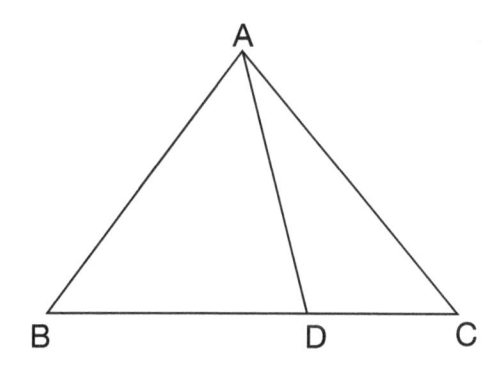

If $|AD| = |BD|$

$m(\widehat{ABD}) = 70$

$m(\widehat{BCA}) = 30$

What is the angle of $\angle(DAC)$?

A) 3°

B) 5°

C) 10°

D) 15°

7.
$$\triangle = x^2 - 2x + 1$$
$$\bigcirc = x^2 - 1$$

From the above if $\bigcirc = \triangle$, then find x.

A) 1

B) 2

C) 3

D) 4

8.

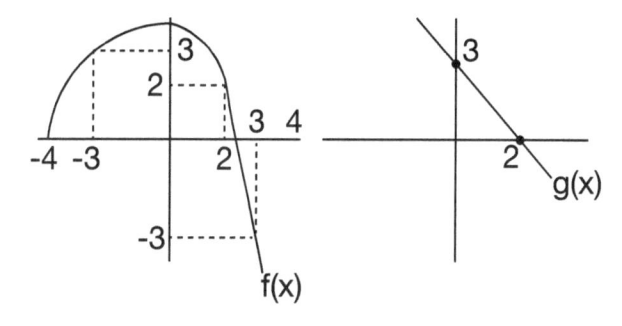

f and g are two functions and their graph is given above.

What is the solution of $f(g(4)) + f(3)$?

A) −2

B) −1

C) 0

D) 1

9. Find $\cos 30° \cdot \sin 60° \cdot \tan 60°$?

A) $\dfrac{\sqrt{3}}{3}$

B) $\dfrac{3}{4}$

C) $\sqrt{3}$

D) $\dfrac{3\sqrt{3}}{4}$

10.

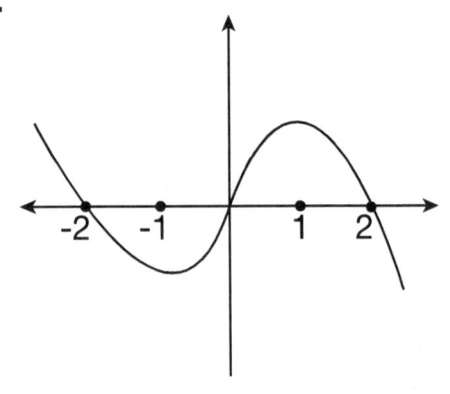

Which of the following could be the equation of the graph above?

A) $x(x-2)(x+2)$

B) $x(x-2)^2$

C) $x(x+2)^2$

D) $(x-2)(x+2)$

11.

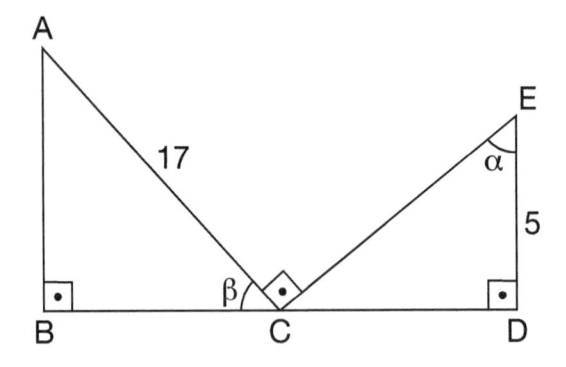

If $AB \perp BC$
$ED \perp CD$
$AC \perp CE$
$|BD| = 27$
$|AB| = 8$
$|AC| = 17$
$|ED| = 5$

From the above triangles, find $\sin \alpha \cdot \cot \beta$?

A) $\dfrac{29}{45}$

B) $\dfrac{45}{29}$

C) $\dfrac{26}{45}$

D) $\dfrac{45}{26}$

MATH PRACTICE TEST II
35 Minutes - 22 Questions
MODULE II

12.

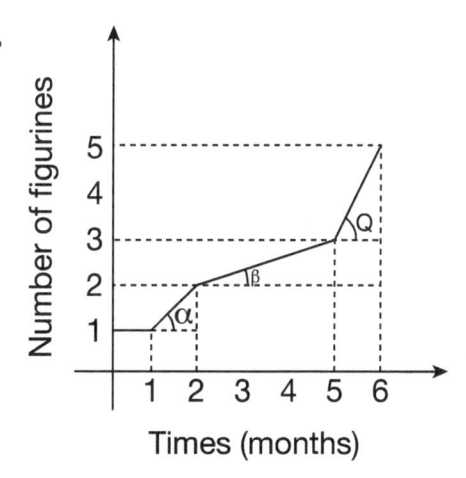

On what interval did the number of figurines increases the fastest?

A) Between 1 and 2 months
B) Between 2 and 5 months
C) Between 1 and 1 months
D) Between 5 and 6 months

13.

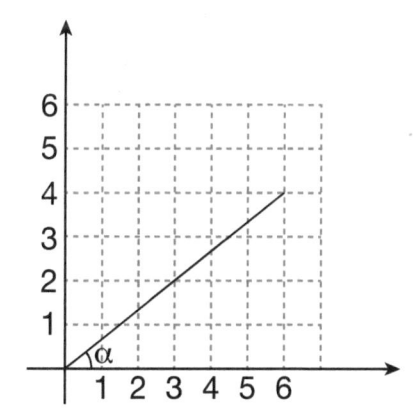

What is the equation of the function?

A) $y = 2x$
B) $y = \frac{2}{3}x$
C) $y = x + 7$
D) $y = 2x + 3$

14. The width of the rectangular dance floor is $x + 8$ feet. The length of the floor is 3 feet longer than it is wide. Which of the following expresses the area in terms of x?

A) $3x^2 + 7$
B) $8x^2 + 23x + 16$
C) $x^2 + 19x + 88$
D) $x^2 + 23x + 17$

15. $\quad ax^3 + bx^2 + cx + d = 0$

In the equation above, a,b,c and d are constants. If the equation roots are −2, 4 and −7, which of the following is a factor of $ax^3 + bx^2 + cx + d$?

A) $x - 2$
B) $x + 4$
C) $x + 7$
D) $x - 7$

16. $\quad f(x) = (x-4)^2 + 11$
$\quad g(x) = 2x + 2.$

What is one possible value of $f(a) = g(a)$?

A) 1
B) 2
C) 3
D) 5

43

MATH PRACTICE TEST II
35 Minutes - 22 Questions
MODULE II

17. $[\{(a+b) \div c\} \cdot d] - e = 3$

In the above equations, if $a = 12$, $b = 18$, $c = 10$ and $d = 3$, then find the value of e.

A) 3

B) 6

C) 9

D) 12

Use the following graph to answer questions 18 and 19.

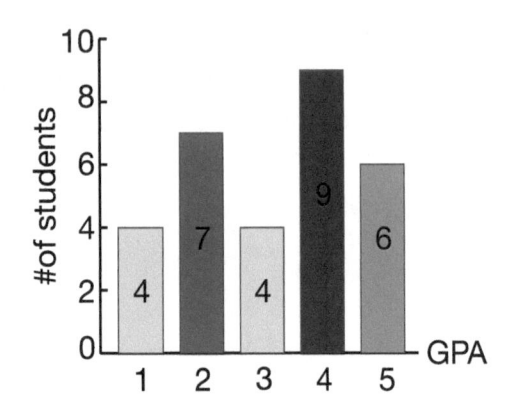

The graph given above is about the number of students and their GPA.

18. What percent of students have a GPA of 5.0?

A) 15

B) 20

C) 25

D) 30

19. The following table shows 2019 salaries for four soccer players. What is the difference from highest salary to lowest salary?

Player A	3.41×10^8
Player B	2.20×10^7
Player C	2.23×10^7
Player D	3.23×10^8

20. Two numbers have a ratio of 5 to 2. If they are positive numbers and differ by 15, what is the value of the smaller number?

21. An investment of $600 increases at a rate of 4% per year. Find the value of investment after 12 years. (Round your answer to the nearest dollar).

22. In college, next year's tuition will increase by 15% per credit. If this year's tuition in college was $660, what will it be next year?

PRACTICE TEST II ANSWER SHEET
MODULE II

1. Ⓐ Ⓑ Ⓒ Ⓓ
2. Ⓐ Ⓑ Ⓒ Ⓓ
3. Ⓐ Ⓑ Ⓒ Ⓓ
4. Ⓐ Ⓑ Ⓒ Ⓓ
5. Ⓐ Ⓑ Ⓒ Ⓓ
6. Ⓐ Ⓑ Ⓒ Ⓓ
7. Ⓐ Ⓑ Ⓒ Ⓓ
8. Ⓐ Ⓑ Ⓒ Ⓓ
9. Ⓐ Ⓑ Ⓒ Ⓓ
10. Ⓐ Ⓑ Ⓒ Ⓓ
11. Ⓐ Ⓑ Ⓒ Ⓓ
12. Ⓐ Ⓑ Ⓒ Ⓓ
13. Ⓐ Ⓑ Ⓒ Ⓓ
14. Ⓐ Ⓑ Ⓒ Ⓓ
15. Ⓐ Ⓑ Ⓒ Ⓓ
16. Ⓐ Ⓑ Ⓒ Ⓓ
17. Ⓐ Ⓑ Ⓒ Ⓓ
18. Ⓐ Ⓑ Ⓒ Ⓓ

19.
20.
21.
22.

PRACTICE TEST II
MODULE I ANSWER KEY

1)	B
2)	B
3)	D
4)	C
5)	C
6)	A
7)	D
8)	C
9)	B
10)	C
11)	B
12)	B
13)	B
14)	A
15)	B
16)	36
17)	B
18)	C
19)	81.5
20)	3
21)	−2
22)	19

PRACTICE TEST II
MODULE I SOLUTIONS

1. $\left(x+\dfrac{x}{2}\right)^2 = \left(x+\dfrac{x}{2}\right)\cdot\left(x+\dfrac{x}{2}\right)$ (Use the foil method)

$= x^2 + \dfrac{x^2}{2} + \dfrac{x^2}{2} + \dfrac{x^2}{4}$

$= x^2 + x^2 + \dfrac{x^2}{4}$

$= 2x^2 + \dfrac{x^2}{4}$

$= \dfrac{9x^2}{4}$

Correct Answer : B

2. $\sqrt{2} \cong 1.21$

$\sqrt{8} \cong 2.8$

$1.4 < x < 2.8$

Choice B is between $1.4 < x < 2.8$

Correct Answer : B

3.

	liters pure water	% water	total liters
80% water	x	.80	.80x
30% water	40	.30	.30(40)=12
60% water	x + 40	.60	.60(x+40)

From the last column, you get the equation
$0.80x + 12 = 0.6(x + 40)$ Solve for x.

$0.80x + 12 = 0.6x + 24$

$0.80x - 0.6x = 24 - 12$

$0.2x = 12$

$2x = 120$

$x = 60$ liters.

Correct Answer : D

4. $2a + 3b = 18 \longrightarrow$ Multily by(−)then elemenation method to find a and b.

$-2a - 3b = -18$

$+\underline{3b - 5a = 11}$

$-7a = -7$

a = 1. Plug in one of the above equations and find b.

$2(1) + 3b = 18$

$2 + 3b = 18$

$3b = 16$

$b = 16/3$

$a - b = 1 - \dfrac{16}{3} = \dfrac{-13}{3}$

Correct Answer : C

5. Increasing = 168,000 − 120,000 = 48,000

Percentage of the increase

$= \dfrac{48,000}{120,00} = \dfrac{48 \div 6}{120 \div 6} = \dfrac{8 \times 5}{20 \times 5} = \dfrac{40}{100} = 40\%$

Correct Answer : C

6. $\dfrac{2}{x-3} = \dfrac{5}{2x-7}$ (Cross multiply)

$2(2x - 7) = 5(x - 3)$

$4x - 14 = 5x - 15$

$-14 + 15 = 5x - 4x$

$1 = x$

Correct Answer : A

PRACTICE TEST II
MODULE I SOLUTIONS

7. $x^3 = 64$,

$x^3 = 4^3$

$x = 4$, then $x^2 = 4^2 = 16$

Correct Answer : D

8. Eggs ⟶ 8x2 = 16 = 2^4

Milk ⟶ 4x2^2 = 16 = 2^4

End of the shopping he pays total = $2^4 + 2^4 = 2^a$

$2^4 (1+1) = 2^a$

$2^4 \cdot 2^1 = 2^a$

$2^5 = 2^a$, a = 5

Correct Answer : C

9. $6^{1/3} = 2^{1/3} \cdot 3^{1/3}$, then

$$\frac{2^{1/2} \cdot 2^{1/3} \cdot 3^{1/3}}{3^{1/3} \cdot 2^{-1/6}} = \frac{2^{\frac{1}{2}} \cdot 2^{\frac{1}{3}}}{2^{\frac{-1}{6}}} = \frac{2^{\frac{5}{6}}}{2^{\frac{-1}{6}}} = 2^{\frac{5}{6}+\frac{1}{6}}$$

$$= 2^{\frac{6}{6}} = 2^1$$

Correct Answer : B

10.

24 feet [rectangle] 32 feet

The Perimeter of the garden is 2(24 + 32) = 112 feet

GCF of (24, 32) = 8 feet

Number of trees is $\frac{112}{8} = 14$

He pays at least 14x5 = $70.

Correct Answer : C

11. If a is even number, and then a + 2 and a + 4 are also even number.

a + a + 2 + a + 4 = 42

3a + 6 = 42

3a = 36

a = 12

Half of smallest number : $\frac{12}{2} = 6$

Correct Answer : B

12. Since C is the center

Arc BD = 90°

$a = \frac{90°}{2} = 45°$

Correct Answer : B

48

PRACTICE TEST II
MODULE I SOLUTIONS

13. $\dfrac{x^2}{9} - \dfrac{y^2}{4} = \left(\dfrac{x}{3} - \dfrac{y}{2}\right) \cdot \left(\dfrac{x}{3} + \dfrac{y}{2}\right)$

Correct Answer : B

14. $\dfrac{3x + 15 - 8}{7} = \dfrac{17 - 6 + x}{5}$

$\dfrac{3x + 7}{7} = \dfrac{11 + x}{5}$ (Cross multiply)

$5(3x + 7) = 7(11 + x)$

$15x + 35 = 77 + 7x$

$15x - 7x = 77 - 35$

$8x = 42$

$x = \dfrac{42}{8} = \dfrac{21}{4}$

Correct Answer : A

15. $\left(\dfrac{1+i}{1-i}\right)^{2018}$

$= \left(\dfrac{(1+i)(1+i)}{(1-i)1+i}\right)^{2018}$

$= \left(\dfrac{1+i+i+i^2}{1-i^2}\right)^{2018}$

$= \left(\dfrac{1+2i-1}{1+1}\right)^{2018} = \left(\dfrac{2i}{2}\right)^{2018}$

$= i^{2018}$

$= (i^2)^{1009} = (-1)^{1009} = -1$

Correct Answer : B

16. $3\alpha + 5\alpha = 96°$

$8\alpha = 96° \rightarrow \alpha = 12° \rightarrow 3\alpha = 3 \cdot 12 = 36°$

Correct Answer : 36°

17. $x^2 + x - 12 = 0$

$(x - 3)(x + 4) = 0$

$x - 3 = 0$, then $x = 3$

or

$x + 4 = 0$, then $x = -4$

The sum of the solutions $3 - 4 = -1$

Correct Answer : B

18. $2a - 3b = 12 \rightarrow$ multiply all equation by 5

$3a + 5b = 18 \rightarrow$ multiply all equation by 3

$10a - 15b = 60$

$+\ \ 9a + 15b = 54$

$\overline{}$

$19a = 114$

$a = 6$

$b = 0$

$a - b = 6 - 0 = 6$

Correct Answer : C

PRACTICE TEST II
MODULE I SOLUTIONS

19. Mean (average)

$$= \frac{88 + 85 + 95 + 66 + 75 + 80}{6}$$

$$= 81.5$$

Correct Answer : 81.5

20. $f(x) = x^2 - 2cx + 8$, if $f(x)$ polynomial is divisible by $x - 4$ then

$x - 4 = 0, x = 4$

$f(4) = 4^2 - 2c(4) + 8$

$0 = 4^2 - 2c(4) + 8$

$0 = 16 - 8c + 8$

$0 = 24 - 8c$

$8c = 24$

$c = 3$

Correct Answer : 3

21. If $x = 1 - \sqrt{3}$ and $y = 1 + \sqrt{3}$, then

$x \cdot y = (1 - \sqrt{3}) \cdot (1 + \sqrt{3})$

$= 1 - 3$

$= -2$

Correct Answer : −2

22. $x^2 + ax - 10 = (x - 1) \cdot (bx + c)$

$x^2 + ax - 10 = bx^2 + cx - bx - c$

$x^2 = x^2 b$, $b = 1$

$ax = x(c - b)$, $a = c - b$

$-10 = -c$, $c = 10$

$a = c - b$

$a = 10 - 1 = 9$

$a + c = 9 + 10 = 19$

Correct Answer : B

PRACTICE TEST II
MODULE II ANSWER KEY

1)	A
2)	B
3)	B
4)	C
5)	A
6)	C
7)	A
8)	C
9)	D
10)	A
11)	D

12)	D
13)	B
14)	C
15)	C
16)	D
17)	B
18)	B
19)	3.19x10
20)	10
21)	$961
22)	$759

PRACTICE TEST II
MODULE II SOLUTIONS

1. $\dfrac{\sqrt{3}\cdot\sqrt[3]{27}}{\sqrt[3]{8}\cdot\sqrt{2}} = \dfrac{\sqrt{3}\cdot\sqrt[3]{3^3}}{\sqrt[3]{2^3}\cdot\sqrt{2}} = \dfrac{\sqrt{3}\cdot 3}{2\sqrt{2}} = \dfrac{3}{2\sqrt{2}}$

$= \dfrac{3\cdot(\sqrt{2})}{2\sqrt{2}\cdot(\sqrt{2})} = \dfrac{3\sqrt{2}}{4}$

Correct Answer : A

2. $A = \{-7, -6, -5, -4, -3, -2, -1, 0, 1, 2, 3, 4, 5, 6\}$
$B = \{-9, -7, -5, -3, -1, 3, 5, 7, 9\}$
$s(A \cap B) = \{-7, -5, -3, -1, 3, 5\}$

Correct Answer : B

3. Julia ⟶ 60%
Mike ⟶ 30%
Peter ⟶ 10%
Julia ⟶ $500 \cdot \dfrac{60}{100} = 300$ votes

Mike ⟶ $500 \cdot \dfrac{30}{100} = 150$ votes

Diffference between Julia and Mike
$300 - 150 = 150$ votes.

Correct Answer : B

4. $f(x) = 3x - 6$
$f(x) = 3x - 6 \rightarrow f(2) = 3\cdot 2 - 6 = 0$
Inverse function:
$y = 3x - 6$ (add 6 in both side)
$y + 6 = 3x$ (divided by 3 both side)
$\dfrac{y+6}{3} = x$ (change x to y for find inverse)

$f^{-1}(x) = \dfrac{x+6}{3} \rightarrow f^{-1}(3) = \dfrac{3+6}{3} = \dfrac{9}{3} = 3$

$f(2) + f^{-1}(3) = 0 + 3 = 3$

Correct Answer : C

5. Probability of the selected odd:

$= \dfrac{P\,odd\,numbers}{total}$

$= \dfrac{5}{10} = \dfrac{1}{2}$

Correct Answer : A

6.

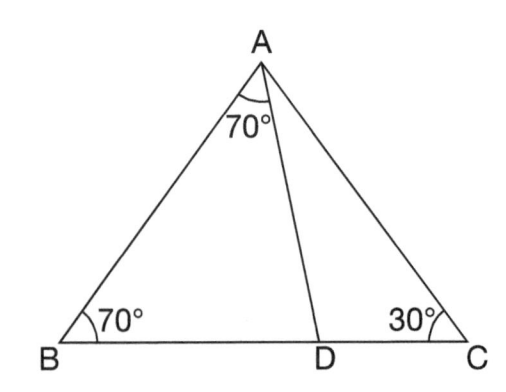

$140 + 30 = 170$
$\widehat{DAC} = 180 - 170$
$\widehat{DAC} = 10$

Correct Answer : C

PRACTICE TEST II
MODULE II SOLUTIONS

7. If $\bigcirc = \triangle$, then

$x^2 - 2x + 1 = x^2 - 1$

$-2x + 1 = -1$

$-2x = -2$

$x = 1$

Correct Answer : A

8. $g(x) = \dfrac{x}{2} + \dfrac{y}{3} = 1 \Longrightarrow 3x + 2y = 6$

$y = g(x) = \dfrac{6 - 3x}{2}$

$g(4) = \dfrac{6 - 12}{2} = -3$

$f(-3) = 3$

$f(3) = -3$

$f(g(4)) + f(3)$

$= 3 - 3$

$= 0$

Correct Answer : C

9. $\cos 30° \cdot \sin 60° \cdot \tan 60°$

$= \dfrac{\sqrt{3}}{2} \cdot \dfrac{\sqrt{3}}{2} \cdot \sqrt{3}$

$= \dfrac{3\sqrt{3}}{4}$

Correct Answer : D

10. Function graph intersect to x line three different points which are $-2, 0, 2$

So, equation has to be $f(x) = x(x - 2) \cdot (x + 2)$

Correct Answer : A

11. We know $|BD| = 27, |BC| = 15$

$|CD| = 27 - 15 = 12$ then $|CE| = 13$

$\sin\alpha = \dfrac{12}{13}$

$\cot\beta = \dfrac{15}{8}$

$\sin\alpha \cdot \cot\beta = \dfrac{12}{13} \cdot \dfrac{15}{8} = \dfrac{45}{26}$

Correct Answer : D

12. A) Between 1 and 2 months $\tan\alpha = 1$,

B) Between 2 and 5 months $\tan\beta = \dfrac{1}{3}$,

C) Between 1 and 1 months $\tan\alpha = 1$,

D) Between 5 and 6 months $\tan Q = 2$

Correct Answer : D

13. $\tan\alpha = \dfrac{2}{3}$

$(0, 0)$ is satisfied;

$y - 0 = \dfrac{2}{3}(x - 0)$

$y = \dfrac{2}{3}x$

Correct Answer : B

PRACTICE TEST II
MODULE II SOLUTIONS

14. $(x + 8) \cdot (x + 11)$

$x^2 + 19x + 88$

Correct Answer : C

15. $f(x) = t(x + 2)(x - 4)(x + 7)$

So, $x + 7$ is a factor of $f(x)$.

Correct Answer : C

16. $f(a) = (a - 4)^2 + 11$

$g(a) = 2a + 2$

If $f(a) = g(a) \implies (a - 4)^2 + 11 = 2a + 2$

$a^2 - 8a + 16 + 11 = 2a + 2$

$a^2 - 10a + 25 = 0$

$(a - 5)^2 = 0$

$a = 5$

Correct Answer : D

17. $[\{(a+b) \div c\} \cdot d] - e = 3$

$[\{(12+18) \div 10\} \cdot 3] - e = 3$

$3 \cdot 3 - e = 3$

$9 - 3 = e$

$6 = e$

Correct Answer : B

18. total students: 30

total 5th grade: 6

% of 5th grade $= \dfrac{6}{30} = \dfrac{1}{5}$

$= 20\%$

Correct Answer : B

PRACTICE TEST II
MODULE II SOLUTIONS

19. Highest salary = Player A = 3.41×10^8

Lowest salary = Player B = 2.20×10^7

Difference from highest salary to lowest salary:

$3.41 \times 10^8 - 2.20 \times 10^7$

$= 10^7 (34.1 - 2.20)$

$= 31.9 \times 10^7 = 3.19 \times 10^8$

Correct Answer : 3.19×10^8

20. If two numbers have a ratio of 5 to 2, and they are positive integers, then can be represented by 5x and 2x.

Since they differ by 15:

$5x - 2x = 15$

$3x = 15$

$x = 5$.

Smaller number = $2x = 2 \cdot 5 = 10$

Bigger number = $5x = 5 \cdot 5 = 25$

Value of smaller number is 10.

Correct Answer : 10

21. $A = P(1 + r)^t$

$P = \$600$

$r = 0.04$

$t = 12$ years

$A = P(1 + r)^t$

$A = \$600(1 + 0.04)^{12}$

$A = \$600(1.04)^{12}$

$A = \$960.61...$

$A = \$961$

Correct Answer : $961

22. Increasing tuition $\$660 \cdot \dfrac{15}{100} = \dfrac{9900}{100} = \$99$

Next year tuition total = $\$660 + \$99 = \$759$

Correct Answer : $759

REFERENCE SHEET

Directions

For each question from 1 to 17, solve each problem, choose the best answer from the choices provided, and fill in the corresponding bubble on your answer sheet.

For questions 18 to 22, solve the problem and enter your answer in the grid on the answer sheet.

Refer to the directions before question 18 for how to enter your answers in the grid. You may use any available space for scratch work.

REFERENCE

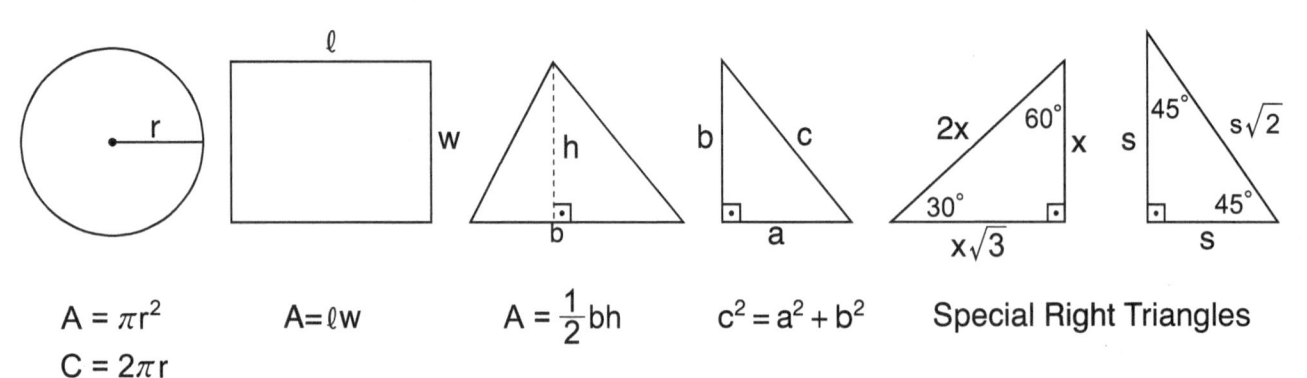

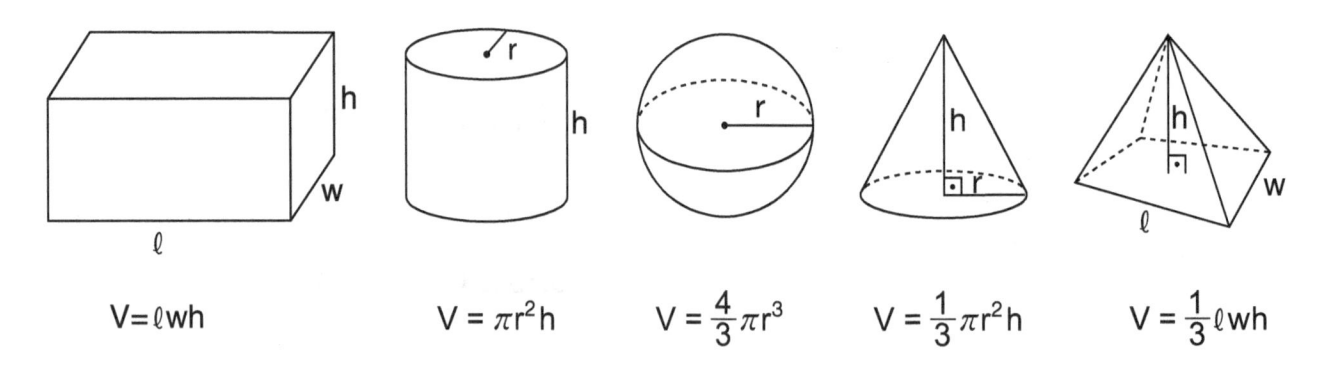

$A = \pi r^2$
$C = 2\pi r$

$A = \ell w$

$A = \frac{1}{2}bh$

$c^2 = a^2 + b^2$

Special Right Triangles

$V = \ell w h$

$V = \pi r^2 h$

$V = \frac{4}{3}\pi r^3$

$V = \frac{1}{3}\pi r^2 h$

$V = \frac{1}{3}\ell w h$

The number of degrees in a circle is 360.

The number of radians in a circle is 2π.

The sum of the measures in degrees of the angles of a triangle is 180.

MATH PRACTICE TEST III
35 Minutes - 22 Questions
MODULE I

1. If $x^3 = 64$, then find x^2.

A) 2

B) 4

C) 8

D) 16

2. If $4^{2x-3} = 8^{3x-7}$, then what is the value of x?

A) 1

B) 2

C) 3

D) 4

3. If $\frac{x}{y} = \frac{a}{b} = \frac{2}{3}$ and $y^2 - b^2 = 27$, then what is the value of $x^2 - a^2$?

A) 12

B) 20

C) 24

D) 25

4. Let D, L and M be sets.

$D = \{a, b, c, d, e\}$

$L = \{b, c, e, q, r\}$

$M = D \cap L$ is given. According to these sets which of the following is equal to set $L \cup (D \cap M)$?

A) D

B) L

C) $M \cup D$

D) $L \cup D$

5. $\frac{2x-6}{4} = \frac{3x-5}{7}$

What is the solution to the equation above?

A) 5

B) 8

C) 11

D) 22

MATH PRACTICE TEST III
35 Minutes - 22 Questions
MODULE I

6. $$\frac{|k+m|-|-2m|+|m-k|}{m-|k|}$$

From the above equation, if $0 > k > m$, what is the solution of the equation?

A) 2m

B) k

C) m + k

D) 0

7. If $y - 3x = 10$, then which of the following is equal to $6x$?

A) y − 5

B) 2y − 5

C) 2y − 20

D) 2y + 20

8.

X	1	2	3	4	5
Y	$\frac{9}{2}$	$\frac{13}{2}$	$\frac{17}{2}$	$\frac{21}{2}$	$\frac{25}{2}$

Which of the following equations relates y to x for the values in the table above? (In the x−y plane)

A) $\frac{3x}{2}+4$

B) $7x+\frac{81}{4}$

C) $\frac{x}{2}+9$

D) $2x+\frac{5}{2}$

9. If $a = 1 - 5i$ and $b = 1 + 5i$, then which of the following is equal to $a \cdot b$?

A) 10

B) 15

C) 25

D) 26

10.

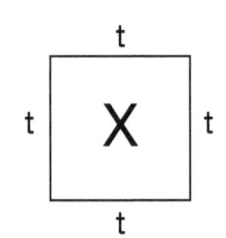

Area of square X is between 102 to 133.

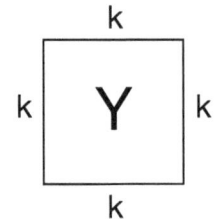

Area of square Y is between 244 to 283.

The side lengths and their area values are given above. If each side of the square has an integers value, what is the sum of $k + t$?

A) 25

B) 27

C) 30

D) 35

58

MATH PRACTICE TEST III
35 Minutes - 22 Questions
MODULE I

Answer the following two questions according to the chart given below.

Subject	Correct	Incorrect
Math	120	40
Physics	60	15
Biology	45	15

The chart is about Frank's test correct and incorrect answers for each subject.

11. What is the percentage of correct answers of all math questions?

A) 50

B) 60

C) 75

D) 80

12. The following formula calculates the test correction average.

(Correct answers−incorrect answers) *2

Find the rate of $\dfrac{(Phy_{avg} + Bio_{avg})}{Math_{avg}}$.

A) $\dfrac{4}{5}$

B) $\dfrac{2}{3}$

C) $\dfrac{12}{13}$

D) $\dfrac{15}{16}$

13. The range of the polynomial function f is the set of real numbers less than or equal to 2. If the zeros of f are −5 and 3, which of the following could be the graph of y=f(x) in the xy−plane?

A)

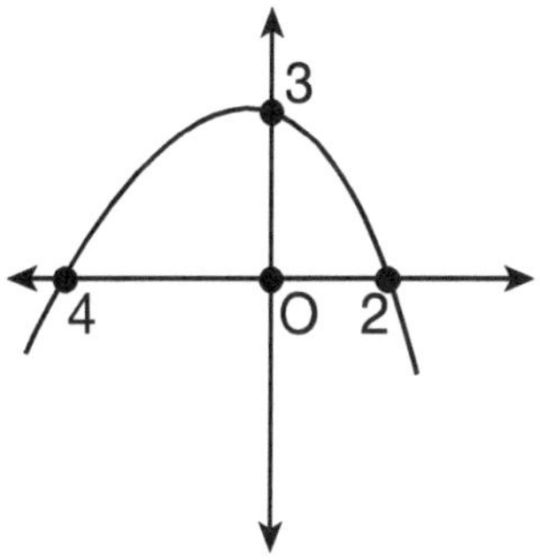

B)

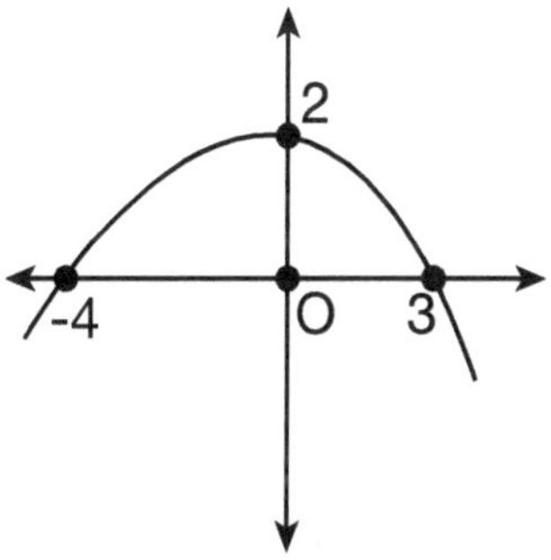

C)

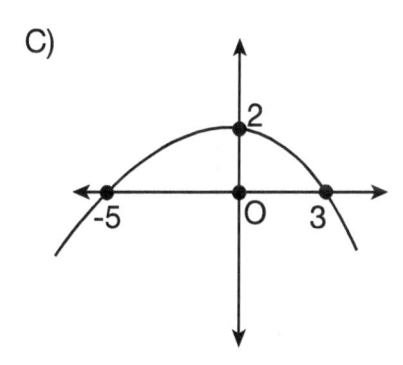

D)

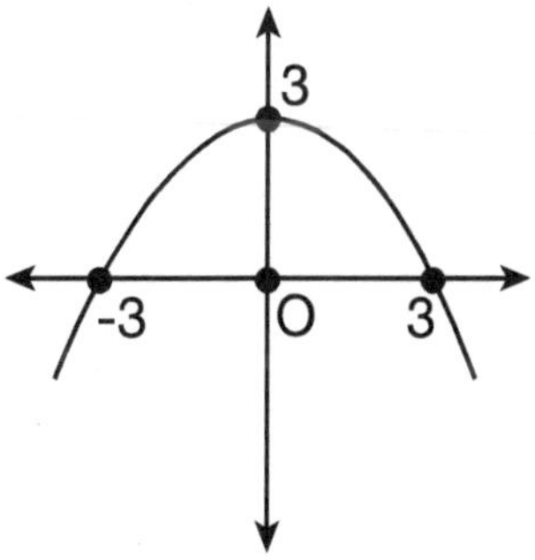

59

MATH PRACTICE TEST III
35 Minutes - 22 Questions
MODULE I

14. A{0, 1, 2, 3, 4, 5, 6, 7, 8, 9}

What is the probability of selecting an even number in set A?

A) $\frac{1}{2}$

B) $\frac{3}{4}$

C) $\frac{5}{6}$

D) $\frac{2}{3}$

15.

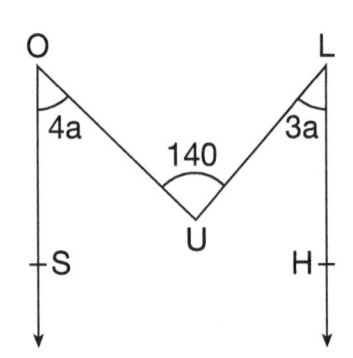

OS // LH

m($\widehat{SOU}$) = 4a, ∠(ULH) = 3a, and ∠(OUL) = 140

So what is the value of 2a?

A) 30

B) 40

C) 50

D) 80

16. If x and y are positive integers and, $\sqrt{x} = y^3 = 8$, then which of the following is the value of $x - y$?

17. On the xy coordinate grid, a line K contains the points (1,3) and (−2,4). If the line L is parallel to line K at (2,1), which of the following is the equation of the line L?

A) $= -\frac{1}{2}x + \frac{5}{3}$

B) $= -\frac{2}{3}x + \frac{5}{3}$

C) $= -\frac{1}{3}x + \frac{3}{5}$

D) $= -\frac{1}{3}x + \frac{5}{3}$

18. x and y are integer numbers.

$-1 < x < 8$

$2 < y < 6$

What is the maximum value of $x^2 + y^2$?

A) 18

B) 36

C) 74

D) 81

MATH PRACTICE TEST III
35 Minutes - 22 Questions
MODULE I

19. What is the value of k if a line that passes through (4, 3) and (−2,k) has a slope of −1?

20.
$$3x + y = 18$$
$$5x - 2y = 8$$

In the system of equations above, what is the value of x + y?

21. The perimeter of a rectangular garden is 43 cm. The width of the garden is 3 cm longer then 4 times the length. What is the length of the garden?

22. $\frac{1}{2}k - 5 + 3k = \frac{3}{2}(k+4)$

What is the value of k in the equation shown above?

PRACTICE TEST III ANSWER SHEET
MODULE I

1. Ⓐ Ⓑ Ⓒ Ⓓ
2. Ⓐ Ⓑ Ⓒ Ⓓ
3. Ⓐ Ⓑ Ⓒ Ⓓ
4. Ⓐ Ⓑ Ⓒ Ⓓ
5. Ⓐ Ⓑ Ⓒ Ⓓ
6. Ⓐ Ⓑ Ⓒ Ⓓ
7. Ⓐ Ⓑ Ⓒ Ⓓ
8. Ⓐ Ⓑ Ⓒ Ⓓ
9. Ⓐ Ⓑ Ⓒ Ⓓ
10. Ⓐ Ⓑ Ⓒ Ⓓ
11. Ⓐ Ⓑ Ⓒ Ⓓ
12. Ⓐ Ⓑ Ⓒ Ⓓ
13. Ⓐ Ⓑ Ⓒ Ⓓ
14. Ⓐ Ⓑ Ⓒ Ⓓ
15. Ⓐ Ⓑ Ⓒ Ⓓ
16. Ⓐ Ⓑ Ⓒ Ⓓ
17. Ⓐ Ⓑ Ⓒ Ⓓ

18.
19.
20.
21.
22.

REFERENCE SHEET

Directions

For each question from 1 to 18, solve each problem, choose the best answer from the choices provided, and fill in the corresponding bubble on your answer sheet.

For questions 19 and 22, solve the problem and enter your answer in the grid on the answer sheet.

Refer to the directions before question 19 for how to enter your answers in the grid. You may use any available space for scratch work.

REFERENCE

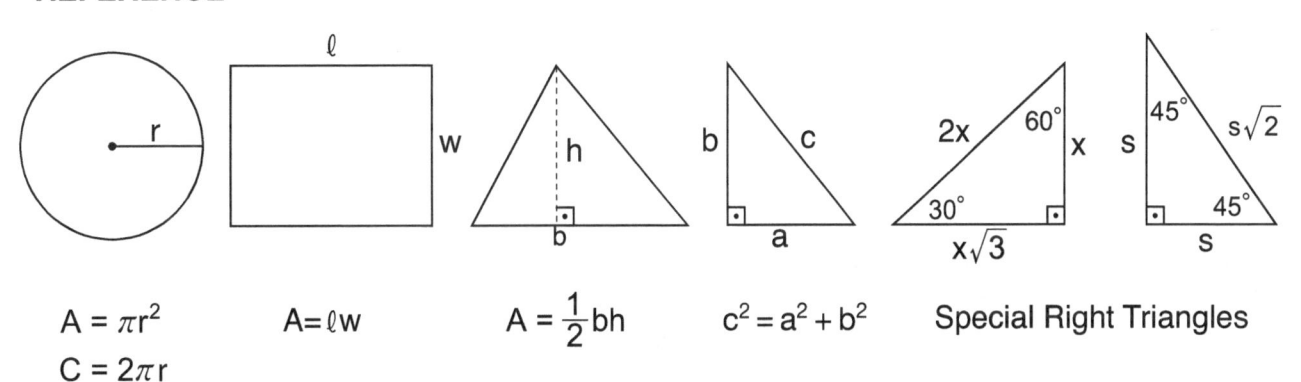

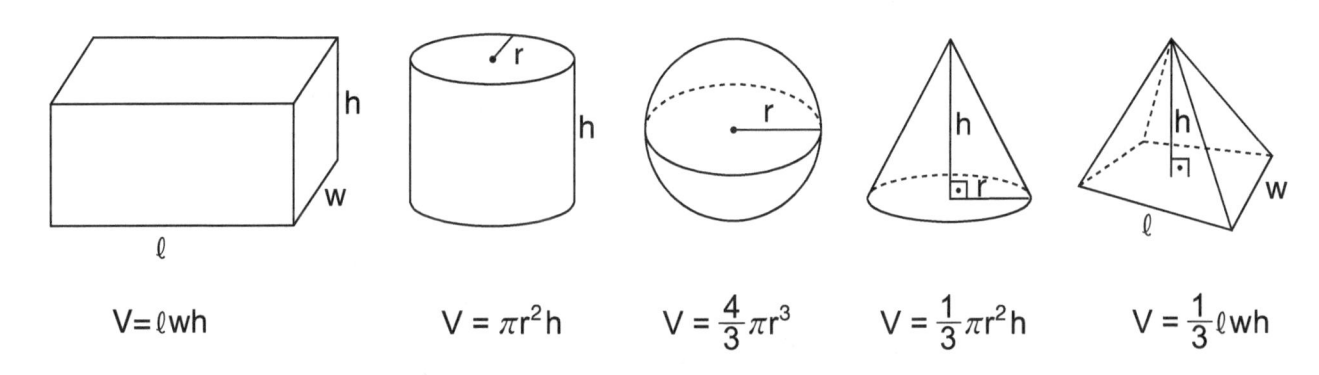

$A = \pi r^2$
$C = 2\pi r$

$A = \ell w$

$A = \frac{1}{2}bh$

$c^2 = a^2 + b^2$

Special Right Triangles

$V = \ell w h$

$V = \pi r^2 h$

$V = \frac{4}{3}\pi r^3$

$V = \frac{1}{3}\pi r^2 h$

$V = \frac{1}{3}\ell w h$

The number of degrees in a circle is 360.

The number of radians in a circle is 2π.

The sum of the measures in degrees of the angles of a triangle is 180.

MATH PRACTICE TEST III
35 Minutes - 22 Questions
MODULE II

1. If $x = -2y + 16$ and $x - 3y = -4$, then what is the value of $\frac{y}{3}$?

A) 3

B) 4

C) $\frac{3}{4}$

D) $\frac{4}{3}$

2.
$$3a = 4b + 4$$
$$6a - 8b = 8$$

How many solutions does the system of equations show above?

A) Zero

B) 1

C) 2

D) Many/infinity

3. $2x - ky + 5 = 0$ if the slope of the equation is $\frac{3}{4}$, what is the value of k?

A) 3

B) 8

C) $\frac{3}{8}$

D) $\frac{8}{3}$

4.
$$f(x) = (x - 4)^2 + 11$$

The function g is defined by $g(x) = 2x + 2$. What is one possible value such that $f(a) = g(a)$?

A) 3

B) 5

C) 7

D) 9

5.
$$f(x) = ax^2 + bx + c.$$

If the function above has roots at $-2, -5$ and $(3,1)$ is satisfied by the function, find a and b?

A) $a = \frac{1}{40}$ $b = \frac{7}{40}$

B) $a = \frac{3}{40}$ $b = \frac{5}{40}$

C) $a = \frac{5}{40}$ $b = \frac{7}{40}$

D) $a = \frac{1}{40}$ $b = \frac{5}{40}$

MATH PRACTICE TEST III
35 Minutes - 22 Questions
MODULE II

6. Melisa has an electronic safe in her office. Her password is a four - digit number and the numbers are different from each other. What is the difference between her largest possible password and smallest possible password?

A) 8642

B) 8640

C) 8634

D) 8562

7. Child: $\left(\frac{1}{3}\right)^{(x-5)}$ cm   Door: $\frac{1}{27}$ cm

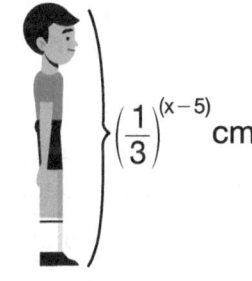

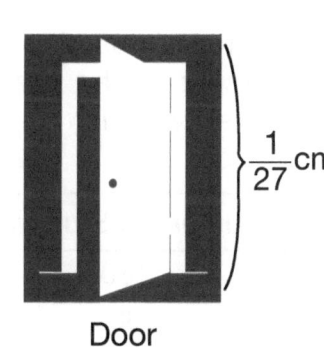

In the figure above if the childs height is less than the door height, what is the smallest value of x?

A) 7

B) 8

C) 9

D) 10

Use the following chart to answer questions 8 and 9.

Dealer Company has three different vehicle colors for cars and bikes. The colors are red, white and blue.

	Car	Bike
Red	30	15
White	40	10
Black	60	5

8. What is the probability of buying a white car from all cars?

A) $\frac{3}{4}$

B) $\frac{4}{13}$

C) 3

D) 4

9. What is the probability of buying a red car from all cars?

A) $\frac{3}{13}$

B) $\frac{13}{3}$

C) 3

D) 4

MATH PRACTICE TEST III
35 Minutes - 22 Questions
MODULE II

10. Simplify $\dfrac{x^2-8x+15}{x^2-9} \div \dfrac{x^2-4x-5}{x^2+3x}$

A) $x-1$

B) $\dfrac{x}{x+1}$

C) $x+1$

D) $\dfrac{x+1}{x-1}$

11. In ABC School, 60 student's favorite subject is science out of 480 students. Find the percent of students whose favorite subject is science?

A) 12.5%

B) 15%

C) 18%

D) 20%

12. Which of following graphs has no correlation?

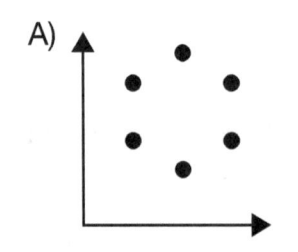

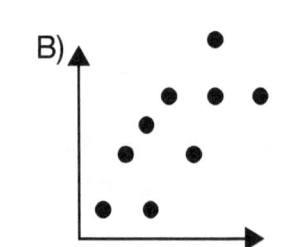

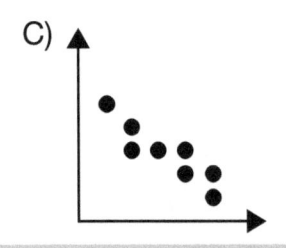

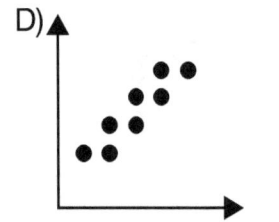

A)

B)

C)

D)

13. For what value of x is the equation $x^2 - 3x - 5 = 0$ true?

A) $\dfrac{3 \pm \sqrt{29}}{2}$

B) $\dfrac{-1 \pm \sqrt{19}}{2}$

C) $\dfrac{-3 \pm \sqrt{26}}{4}$

D) $\dfrac{-3 \pm \sqrt{29}}{6}$

14. The table below shows the results of a survey on how students get to school. A circle graph is used to display the data. What percent of the graph represents the car transportation?

Number of Students	Transportation
180	School Bus
60	Car
20	Walk
40	Bike

A) 20%

B) 30%

C) 45%

D) 50%

MATH PRACTICE TEST III
35 Minutes - 22 Questions
MODULE II

15.

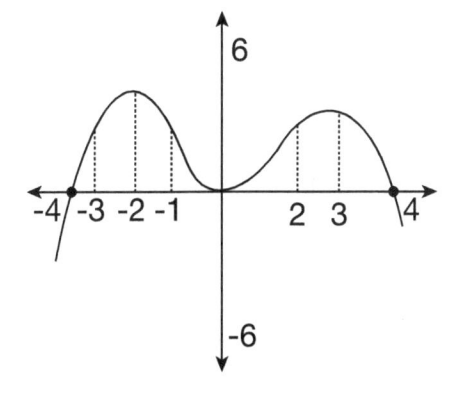

Which of the following could be the equation of the graph above?

A) $x \cdot (x-3) \cdot (x+3)$

B) $x^2 \cdot (x+4) \cdot (x-5)$

C) $x^2 \cdot (x^2 - 16)$

D) $x^2 \cdot (x+4) \cdot (x-3)$

17.

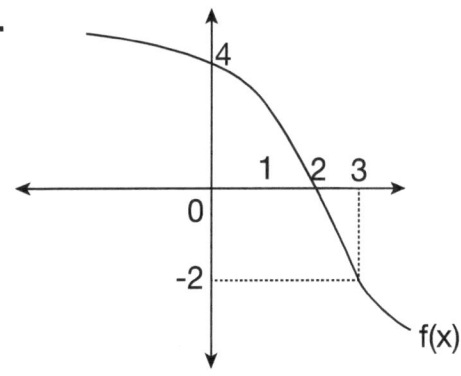

Using the above f(x) function, find the value of $f(0) + f^{-1}(-2) + f(3)$?

A) 5

B) 10

C) 12

D) 16

16.

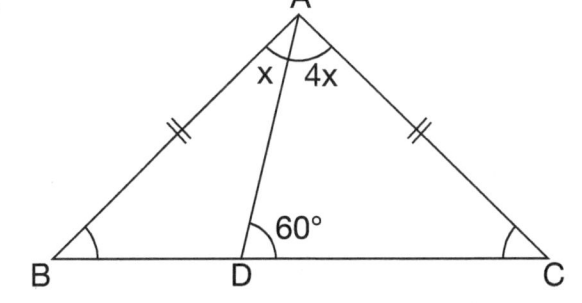

What is the value of x?

A) 10°

B) 20°

C) 30°

D) 40°

18. In a right triangle, one angle measures x°, where $\cos x° = \dfrac{5}{13}$.

What is the $\tan(90 - x°)$?

A) $\dfrac{12}{13}$

B) $\dfrac{5}{12}$

C) $\dfrac{7}{12}$

D) $\dfrac{13}{12}$

MATH PRACTICE TEST III
35 Minutes - 22 Questions
MODULE II

19.

A •——3x-4——• B ——2x——• C ——$x-\frac{1}{2}$——• D

Note: Figure not drawn to scale

on $\overline{AD}$ above, AB = CD. What is the length of $\overline{AD}$?

20. In the xy–plane, the point (3, 5) lies on the graph of the function h. If $h(x) = x^2 - c$, where c is a constant, what is the value of c?

21. $\dfrac{3x-1}{(x-2)^2} - \dfrac{3}{x-2}$

The expression above is equivalent to $\dfrac{k}{(x-2)^2}$, where k is a positive constant and $x \neq 2$. What is the value of k?

22. An airplane traveled 1.5×10^2 miles per hour for 0.5×10^2 hours. How far did the airplane travel?

PRACTICE TEST III ANSWER SHEET
MODULE II

1. Ⓐ Ⓑ Ⓒ Ⓓ   7. Ⓐ Ⓑ Ⓒ Ⓓ   13. Ⓐ Ⓑ Ⓒ Ⓓ
2. Ⓐ Ⓑ Ⓒ Ⓓ   8. Ⓐ Ⓑ Ⓒ Ⓓ   14. Ⓐ Ⓑ Ⓒ Ⓓ
3. Ⓐ Ⓑ Ⓒ Ⓓ   9. Ⓐ Ⓑ Ⓒ Ⓓ   15. Ⓐ Ⓑ Ⓒ Ⓓ
4. Ⓐ Ⓑ Ⓒ Ⓓ   10. Ⓐ Ⓑ Ⓒ Ⓓ   16. Ⓐ Ⓑ Ⓒ Ⓓ
5. Ⓐ Ⓑ Ⓒ Ⓓ   11. Ⓐ Ⓑ Ⓒ Ⓓ   17. Ⓐ Ⓑ Ⓒ Ⓓ
6. Ⓐ Ⓑ Ⓒ Ⓓ   12. Ⓐ Ⓑ Ⓒ Ⓓ   18. Ⓐ Ⓑ Ⓒ Ⓓ

19.   20.   21.   22.

PRACTICE TEST III
MODULE I ANSWER KEY

1)	D
2)	C
3)	A
4)	B
5)	C
6)	D
7)	C
8)	D
9)	D
10)	B
11)	C
12)	D
13)	C
14)	A
15)	B
16)	62
17)	D
18)	C
19)	9
20)	10
21)	3.7
22)	5.5

PRACTICE TEST III
MODULE I SOLUTIONS

1. If $x^3 = 64$, then $x^3 = 4^3$, $x = 4$

$x^2 = 4^2 = 16$

Correct Answer : D

2. $4^{2x-3} = 8^{3x-7}$

$2^{2(2x-3)} = 2^{3(3x-7)}$

$2^{4x-6} = 2^{9x-21}$

$4x - 6 = 9x - 21$

$-6 + 21 = 9x - 4x$

$15 = 5x$

$3 = x$

Correct Answer : C

3. $\dfrac{x^2}{y^2} = \dfrac{a^2}{b^2} = \dfrac{4}{9}$ (Cross multiply)

$9x^2 = 4y^2 \longrightarrow y^2 = \dfrac{9x^2}{4}$

$9a^2 = 4b^2 \longrightarrow b^2 = \dfrac{9}{4}a^2$

if $y^2 - b^2 = 27$

$\dfrac{9x^2}{4} - \dfrac{9}{4}a^2 = 27$

$\dfrac{9x^2 - 9a^2}{4} = 27$

$\dfrac{9(x^2 - a^2)}{4} = 27$

$x^2 - a^2 = \dfrac{27 \cdot 4}{9} = 12$

Correct Answer : A

4. $M = D \cap L = \{b, c, e\}$ then $D \cap M = \{b, c, e\}$

So; $L \cup (D \cap M) = \{b, c, e, q, r\} \cup \{b, c, e\} = L$

Correct Answer : B

5. $\dfrac{2x-6}{4} = \dfrac{3x-5}{7}$ (Cross multiply)

$7(2x - 6) = 4(3x - 5)$

$14x - 42 = 12x - 20$

$14x - 12x = 42 - 20$

$2x = 22$

$x = 11$

Correct Answer : C

6. If $m < k < 0$, then

$|k + m| = -k - m$

$|-2m| = -2m$

$|m - k| = -m + k$

$|k| = -k$

$= \dfrac{-k + m + 2m - m + k}{1 + k} = \dfrac{0}{1 + k} = 0$

Correct Answer : D

PRACTICE TEST III
MODULE I SOLUTIONS

7. If $y - 3x = 10$, then $3x = y - 10$

So, $6x = 2(3x) = 2(y-10) = 2y - 20$

Correct Answer : C

8. $\left.\begin{array}{l}\left(1, \dfrac{9}{2}\right) \\ \left(1, \dfrac{13}{2}\right)\end{array}\right\}$ Use this 2 points to find slope.

Slope $= \dfrac{y_2 - y_1}{x_2 - x_1}$

Slope $= \dfrac{\dfrac{13}{2} - \dfrac{9}{2}}{2 - 1} = \dfrac{\dfrac{4}{2}}{2-1} = \dfrac{2}{1} = 2$

Slope point form:

$y - y_1 = m(x - x_1)$

$y - \dfrac{9}{2} = 2(x - 1)$

$y = 2x - 2 + \dfrac{9}{2}$

$y = 2x + \dfrac{5}{2}$

Correct Answer : D

9. $a = 1 - 5i$ and $b = 1 + 5i$, then

$a \cdot b = (1 - 5i) \cdot (1 + 5i)$

$= 1 - 25i^2$

$= 1 + 25$

$= 26$

Correct Answer : D

10. t is one side of square of X

$102 < t^2 < 133$

t must be 11

k is one side of square of Y

$244 < k^2 < 283$

k must be 16

$t + k = 11 + 16 = 27$

Correct Answer : B

11. Total math questions $= 120 + 40$
$= 160$

160 ⨯ 120
100 ⨯ x

$x = \dfrac{100 \cdot 120}{160} = 75\%$

Correct Answer : C

12. $Phy_{avg} = (60 - 15) \times 2 = 90$

$Bio_{avg} = (45 - 15) \times 2 = 60$

$Math_{avg} = (120 - 40) \times 2 = 160$

$\dfrac{(Phy_{avg} + Bio_{avg})}{Math_{avg}} = \dfrac{90 + 60}{160} = \dfrac{15}{16}$

Correct Answer : D

PRACTICE TEST III
MODULE I SOLUTIONS

13. (0, 2) Is satisfied and
x = −5 and x = 3

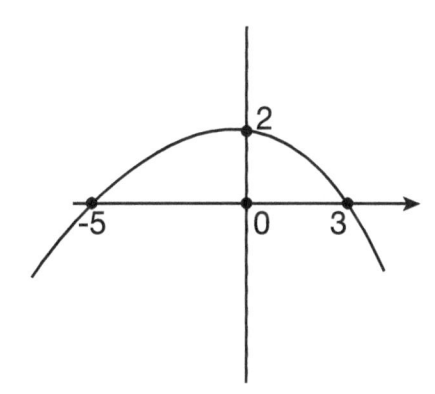

Correct Answer : C

14. Even numbers are 0,2,4,6,and, 8.

Probability of the selecting even number

$= \frac{5}{10} = \frac{1}{2}$

Correct Answer : A

15. Since OS // LH   4a + 3a = 140

7a = 140

a = 20, then   2a = 40

Correct Answer : B

16. If x and y are positive integers and

$\sqrt{x} = y^3 = 8$.

$\sqrt{x} = 8$, then x = ∓64 since

x is positive then x = 64

$y^3 = 8$, then y = 2

x − y = 64 − 2 = 62

Correct Answer : 62

17. (1, 3) and (−2, 4)

Slope $= \frac{y_2 - y_1}{x_2 - x_1}$

$m = \frac{4-3}{-2-1} = -\frac{1}{3}$

If $m_1 // m_2$, then $m_1 = m_2$

$m_2 = -\frac{1}{3}$, (2, 1) → use the point-slope form

$y - y_1 = m(x - x_1)$

$y - 1 = -\frac{1}{3}(x - 2)$

$y - 1 = -\frac{1}{3}x + \frac{2}{3}$

$y = -\frac{1}{3}x + \frac{2}{3} + 1$

$y = -\frac{1}{3}x + \frac{5}{3}$

Correct Answer : D

18. Since x and y are integer numbers.

−1 < x < 8

2 < y < 6

Maximum value of x is: 7

Maximum value of y is: 5

$x^2 + y^2 = 7^2 + 5^2 = 49 + 25 = 74$

Correct Answer : C

PRACTICE TEST III
MODULE I SOLUTIONS

19. (4, 3), (−2, k) and slope = −1

Slope = $\dfrac{y_2 - y_1}{x_2 - x_1}$

Slope = $\dfrac{k-3}{-2-4} = \dfrac{k-3}{-6}$

$-1 = \dfrac{k-3}{-6}$

$6 = k - 3$, $6 + 3 = k$

$9 = k$

Correct Answer : 9

20. $3x + y = 18$ ⟶ multiply all equations by 2

$5x - 2y = 8$ ⟶ keep equation same

$6x + 2y = 36$

$5x - 2y = 8$

+ ─────────

$11x = 44$

$x = 4$, then plug in 4 for x and find y.

$5x - 2y = 8$

$5(4) - 2y = 8$

$20 - 2y = 8$

$20 - 8 = 2y$

$12 = 2y$

$6 = y$

$x + y = 4 + 6 = 10$

Correct Answer : 10

21. Perimeter of a rectangular garden = 43 cm

Perimeter = 2L + 2W = 43cm

$W = 4L + 3$

$2L + 2(4L + 3) = 43$

$2L + 8L + 6 = 43$

$10L = 43 - 6$

$10L = 37$

$L = 3.7$

Correct Answer : 3.7

22. $\dfrac{1}{2}k - 5 + 3k = \dfrac{3}{2}(k + 4)$

$\dfrac{1}{2}k + 3k - 5 = \dfrac{3}{2}k + \dfrac{3(4)}{2}$

$\dfrac{7k}{2} - 5 = \dfrac{3k}{2} + 6$

$\dfrac{7k}{2} - \dfrac{3k}{2} = 6 + 5$

$\dfrac{4k}{2} = 11$

$k = \dfrac{22}{4} = 5.5$

Correct Answer : 5.5

78

PRACTICE TEST III
MODULE II ANSWER KEY

1)	D
2)	D
3)	D
4)	B
5)	A
6)	A
7)	C
8)	B
9)	A
10)	B
11)	A

12)	A
13)	A
14)	A
15)	C
16)	B
17)	A
18)	B
19)	6
20)	4
21)	5
22)	7,500 miles

PRACTICE TEST III
MODULE II SOLUTIONS

1. $x + 2y = 16 \longrightarrow$ multiply by (−) then use substitute method.

$\cancel{-}x - 2y = -16$

$+ \quad x - 3y = -4$

$\overline{-5y = -20}$

$y = 4$, then $\frac{y}{3}$ is $\frac{4}{3}$

Correct Answer : D

2. $3a = 4b + 4 \longrightarrow 3a - 4b = 4$

$6a - 8b = 8 \longrightarrow$ divide by 2 all the equations $\longrightarrow 3a - 4b = 4$

Since both equations are equivalent the system of equations has many/infinitely solutions.

Correct Answer : D

3. $2x - ky + 5 = 0 \longrightarrow$ from this equation the slope is $\frac{2}{k}$.

$\frac{2}{k} = \frac{3}{4}$ (cross multiply)

$3k = 8$

$k = \frac{8}{3}$

Correct Answer : D

4. $f(a) = (a - 4)^2 + 11$

$g(a) = 2a + 2$

If $f(a) = g(a) \Longrightarrow (a - 4)^2 + 11 = 2a + 2$

$a^2 - 8a + 16 + 11 = 2a + 2$

$a^2 - 8a + 27 = 2a + 2$

$a^2 - 10a + 25 = 0$

$(a - 5)^2 = 0$

$a = 5$

Correct Answer : B

5. $f(x) = t(x + 2) \cdot (x + 5)$, and $(3, 1)$ is satisfied that;

$1 = t(3 + 2) \cdot (3 + 5)$

$1 = t \cdot (5) \cdot (8)$

$1 = t \cdot 40$

$t = \frac{1}{40}$

So;

$f(x) = \frac{1}{40} \cdot (x + 2) \cdot (x + 5)$

$\Longrightarrow \frac{1}{40} \cdot (x^2 + 7x + 10)$

$\Longrightarrow \frac{x^2}{40} + \frac{7x}{40} + \frac{1}{4} = ax^2 + bx + c$

$a = \frac{1}{40}, b = \frac{7}{40}$

Correct Answer : A

6. Largest possible password: 9876

Smallest possible password: 1234

$9876 - 1234 = 8642$

Correct Answer : A

PRACTICE TEST III
MODULE II SOLUTIONS

7. $\left(\dfrac{1}{3}\right)^{x-5} < \dfrac{1}{27}$

Since the child height is less than the door height

$3^{-1(x-5)} < 3^{-3}$,

$5 - x < -3$

$8 < x$ smallest possible value of x is 9

Correct Answer : C

8. Probability of buying a white car

$= \dfrac{40}{30+40+60} = \dfrac{40}{130} = \dfrac{4}{13}$

Correct Answer : B

9. Probability of buying a red car

$= \dfrac{30}{30+40+60} = \dfrac{30}{130} = \dfrac{3}{13}$

Correct Answer : A

10. $\dfrac{x^2-8x+15}{x^2-9} \div \dfrac{x^2-4x-5}{x^2+3x}$

$\dfrac{(x-5)(x-3)}{(x-3)(x+3)} \cdot \dfrac{x(x+3)}{(x-5)(x+1)}$

$= \dfrac{x}{x+1}$

Correct Answer : B

11. Percent of students whose favorite subject is science $= \dfrac{60}{480} = \dfrac{1}{8} = 12.5\%$

Correct Answer : A

12. No Correlation

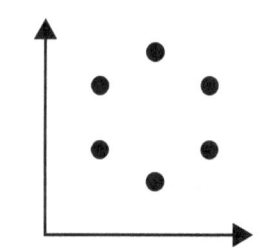

Correct Answer : A

13. $x^2 - 3x - 5 = 0$

$x^2 - 3x = 5$

$\left(x - \dfrac{3}{2}\right)^2 - \dfrac{9}{4} = 5$

$\left(x - \dfrac{3}{2}\right)^2 = \dfrac{29}{4}$

$x - \dfrac{3}{2} = \mp\sqrt{\dfrac{29}{4}}$

$x = \mp\dfrac{\sqrt{29}}{2} + \dfrac{3}{2}$

$x = \dfrac{\mp\sqrt{29}+3}{2}$

Correct Answer : A

PRACTICE TEST III
MODULE II SOLUTIONS

14. $\dfrac{\text{Car}}{\text{Total}} = \dfrac{6\cancel{0}}{30\cancel{0}} = \dfrac{6}{30}$

$= \dfrac{1 \times 20}{5 \times 20} = \dfrac{20}{100}$

$= 20\%$

Correct Answer : A

15. The graph's zeros are $x = 0$, $x = 4$, $x = -4$ but $x = 0$ is twice zeros so;

$f(x) = x^2 \cdot (x - 4) \cdot (x + 4)$

$= x^2 \cdot (x^2 - 16)$

Correct Answer : C

16.

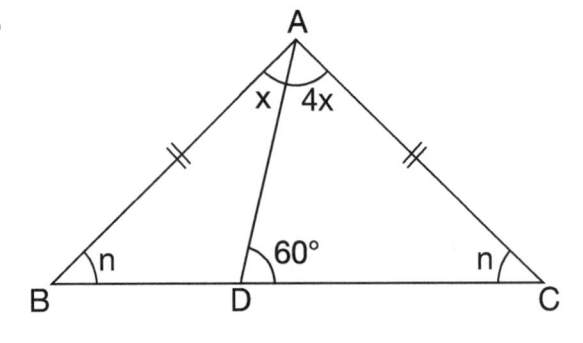

$x + n = 60°$

$5x + 2n = 180°$ $x = 20°$

Correct Answer : B

17. $f(0) = 4$

$f^{-1}(-2) = 3$, then $f(3) = -2$

$f(0) + f^{-1}(2) + f(3) = 4 + 3 - 2 = 5$

Correct Answer : A

18.

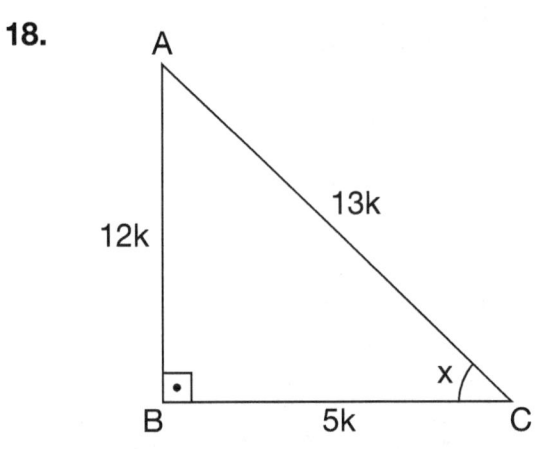

$\tan(90 - x°) = \cot x° = \dfrac{5k}{12k} = \dfrac{5}{12}$

Correct Answer : B

PRACTICE TEST III
MODULE II SOLUTIONS

19. AB = 3x−4

CD = $x - \frac{1}{2}$

If AB = CD, then

$3x - 4 = x - \frac{1}{2}$

$3x - x = 4 - \frac{1}{2}$

$2x = \frac{7}{2}$

$x = \frac{7}{4}$

AD = $3x - 4 + 2x + x - \frac{1}{2}$

AD = $6x - \frac{9}{2}$

AD = $6\left(\frac{7}{4}\right) - \frac{9}{2}$

AD = $\frac{42}{4} - \frac{9}{2} = \frac{42-18}{4}$

AD = $\frac{42-18}{4} = \frac{24}{4} = 6$

Correct Answer : 6

20. $h(x) = x^2 - c$, (3,5) ⟶ plug in this point to function for find c.

$h(3) = 3^2 - c$

$5 = 9 - k$

$c = 9-5$

$c = 4$

Correct Answer : 4

21. $\frac{3x-1}{(x-2)^2} - \frac{3}{x-2} = \frac{k}{(x-2)^2}$ (make their denominators same)

$\frac{3x-1}{(x-2)^2} - \frac{3(x-2)}{(x-2)^2} = \frac{k}{(x-2)^2}$

$\frac{3x-1-3(x-2)}{(x-2)^2} = \frac{k}{(x-2)^2}$ (take out denominators)

$3x - 1 - 3x + 6 = k$

$-1 + 6 = k$

$5 = k$

Correct Answer : 5

22. Distance = Rate x Time

Distance = $(1.5 \times 10^2)(0.5 \times 10^2)$

Distance = 0.75×10^4

Distance = 0.75(10,000)

Distance = 7,500 miles.

Correct Answer : 7,500 miles.

83

REFERENCE SHEET

Directions

For each question from 1 to 17, solve each problem, choose the best answer from the choices provided, and fill in the corresponding bubble on your answer sheet.

For questions 18 to 22, solve the problem and enter your answer in the grid on the answer sheet.

Refer to the directions before question 18 for how to enter your answers in the grid. You may use any available space for scratch work.

REFERENCE

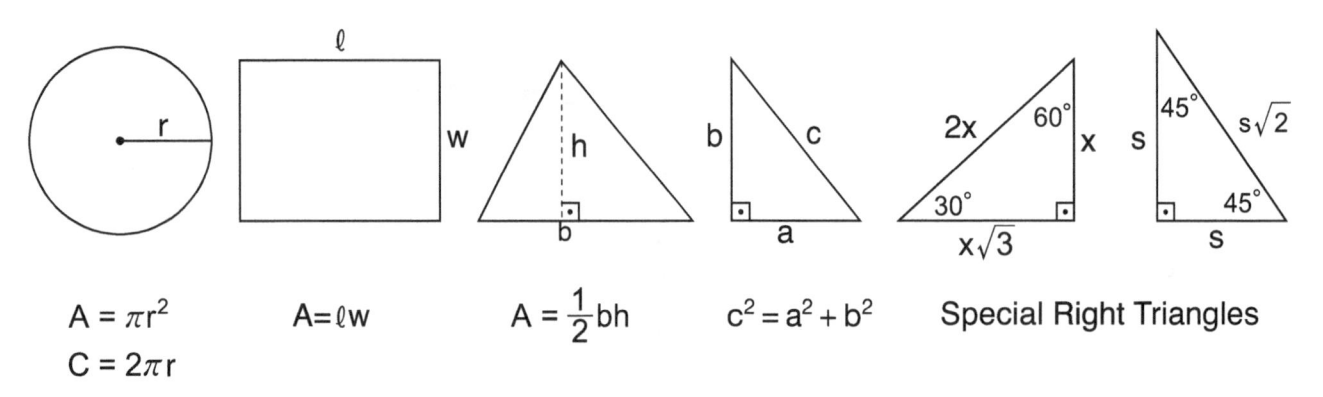

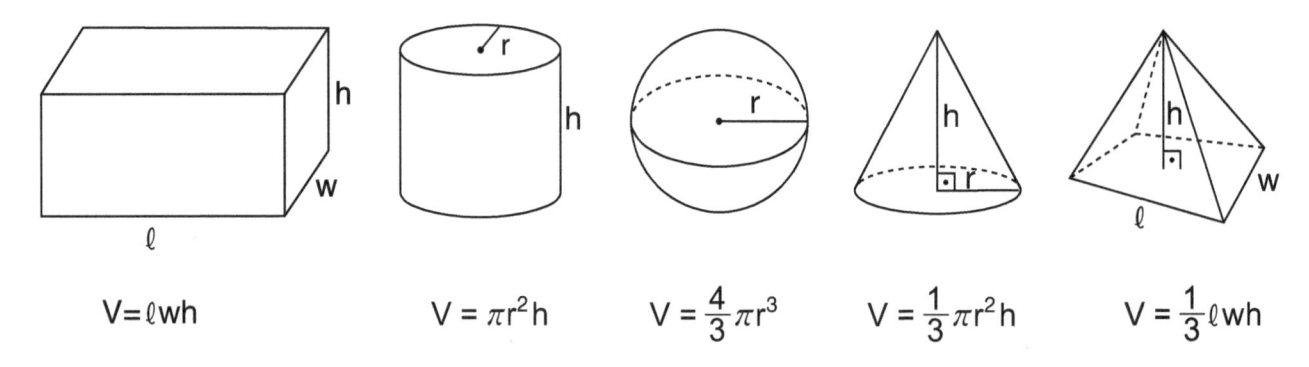

$A = \pi r^2$
$C = 2\pi r$

$A = \ell w$

$A = \frac{1}{2} bh$

$c^2 = a^2 + b^2$

Special Right Triangles

$V = \ell w h$

$V = \pi r^2 h$

$V = \frac{4}{3}\pi r^3$

$V = \frac{1}{3}\pi r^2 h$

$V = \frac{1}{3}\ell w h$

The number of degrees in a circle is 360.

The number of radians in a circle is 2π.

The sum of the measures in degrees of the angles of a triangle is 180.

MATH PRACTICE TEST IV
35 Minutes - 22 Questions
MODULE I

1. If $x^{\frac{1}{3}} = 64$, then find $\frac{x}{2}$.

   A) 2^{15}

   B) 2^{17}

   C) 2^{18}

   D) 2^{20}

2. If $9^{(2x-3)} = 27^{(3x-7)}$, then what is the value of x?

   A) 1

   B) 2

   C) 3

   D) 4

3. $$\frac{x-6}{3} = \frac{2x-7}{4}$$

   What is the solution to the equation above?

   A) -2

   B) -3

   C) $-\frac{2}{3}$

   D) $-\frac{3}{2}$

4. If $3y - \frac{x}{4} = 10$, then which of the following is equal to $\frac{x}{2}$?

   A) $6y - 20$

   B) $3y - 10$

   C) $y - 20$

   D) $6y + 20$

5. Which of the following is equal to $\frac{4}{1+i\sqrt{3}}$?

   A) $1 - i\sqrt{3}$

   B) $1 + i\sqrt{3}$

   C) 1

   D) $3i$

6. $$a^2 - b^2 = 36$$
   $$\frac{1}{a-b} + \frac{1}{a+b} = \frac{2}{9}$$

   From the above equations, if a and b are integers, what is the value of a?

   A) 3

   B) 4

   C) 5

   D) 6

85

MATH PRACTICE TEST IV
35 Minutes - 22 Questions
MODULE I

7. Tricio is $6\frac{3}{4}$ years old, Laurie is $6\frac{1}{2}$ years old, Jim is 6.25 years old. Mark is 6.5 years old. Which two children have the same age?

   A) Laurie and Mark
   B) Tricio and Jim
   C) Mark and Jim
   D) Laurie and Tricio

8. If $A = \sqrt{5}, B = \sqrt{6}, C = 3,$ and $D = \sqrt{20}$, what is the value of $|A-B|+|C-B|+|D-C|$?

   A) $\sqrt{5}$
   B) 0
   C) $-\sqrt{5}$
   D) 6

9. A fitness center has two membership plans. One is a $23 membership fee and $7 per visit and another one is only per visit fees of $13. Which of the following systems of equations can be used to determine the fitness center membership plans?

   A) $y = 7 + 23x$
      $y = 13$
   B) $y = 23 + 7x$
      $y = 13x$
   C) $y = 13$
      $y = 23 + 7x$
   D) $y = 13x$
      $y = 23x + 7$

10. A →(multiply by 6)→ (substract 5)→ (multiply by 2)→ (divided by 7)→ 14

    A number is applied step by step in the direction of arrows and the result is 14. Which of following is true for A?

    A) A is a prime number.
    B) A is a even number.
    C) A is a perfect square.
    D) A is a negative number.

MATH PRACTICE TEST IV
35 Minutes - 22 Questions
MODULE I

11. If x and y are positive integers and

$$y = x^2 + 9$$
$$y = 7x - 3$$

Which of following could be value of x?

A) 2

B) 4

C) 6

D) 8

12.
$$\frac{k}{2km} = \frac{1}{k+m}$$

From the above equation what is the value of m in terms of k?

A) k^2

B) $k^2 + 1$

C) $k^2 - 1$

D) k

13. If x hour is equivalent to y minutes, of the following, which best represents the relationship between x and y?

A) $x = y$

B) $x = 30y$

C) $x = 60y$

D) $x = 120y$

14. $(x - 3)^2 + (y + 7)^2 = 16$

If a circle in the xy–plane has the equation above, what is the radius of the circle?

A) 3

B) 4

C) 5

D) 7

MATH PRACTICE TEST IV
35 Minutes - 22 Questions
MODULE I

15.

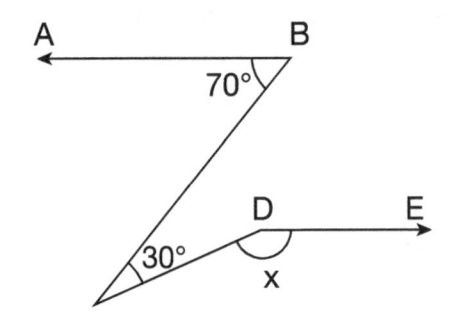

AB // DE

What is the value of x?

A) 120°

B) 140°

C) 150°

D) 160°

16. If x, y and z are real numbers and;

$$x^3 \cdot y^2 > 0$$
$$x^2 \cdot z > 0$$
$$y^3 \cdot z < 0$$

Which of the following must be true?

A) +, +, +

B) −, +, −

C) +, −, −

D) +, −, +

17.

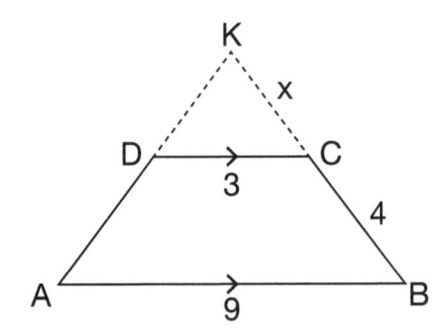

If DC // AB in the above figure, what is the value of x?

A) 2

B) 4

C) 6

D) 8

MATH PRACTICE TEST IV
35 Minutes - 22 Questions
MODULE I

18. If x and y are positive integers and $\sqrt{x} = y^4 = 16$, then which of the following is the value of $x - y$?

19. What is the value of k if a line that passes through $(-7, 3)$ and $(2, k)$ has a slope of 1?

20.
$$\frac{1}{2}x + y = 18$$
$$x - \frac{3}{2}y = 8$$

In the system of equations above, what is the value of $x + y$?

21. Melissa's monthly electrical bill was $125. Due to a rate decrease, her monthly bill is now $110. To the nearest to tenth of a percent, by what percent did the amount of the customers electrical bill decrease?

22.
$$k - 9 + \frac{5k}{2} = \frac{1}{2}k + 7$$

What is the value of k in the equation shown above?

89

PRACTICE TEST IV ANSWER SHEET
MODULE I

1. Ⓐ Ⓑ Ⓒ Ⓓ
2. Ⓐ Ⓑ Ⓒ Ⓓ
3. Ⓐ Ⓑ Ⓒ Ⓓ
4. Ⓐ Ⓑ Ⓒ Ⓓ
5. Ⓐ Ⓑ Ⓒ Ⓓ
6. Ⓐ Ⓑ Ⓒ Ⓓ
7. Ⓐ Ⓑ Ⓒ Ⓓ
8. Ⓐ Ⓑ Ⓒ Ⓓ
9. Ⓐ Ⓑ Ⓒ Ⓓ
10. Ⓐ Ⓑ Ⓒ Ⓓ
11. Ⓐ Ⓑ Ⓒ Ⓓ
12. Ⓐ Ⓑ Ⓒ Ⓓ
13. Ⓐ Ⓑ Ⓒ Ⓓ
14. Ⓐ Ⓑ Ⓒ Ⓓ
15. Ⓐ Ⓑ Ⓒ Ⓓ
16. Ⓐ Ⓑ Ⓒ Ⓓ
17. Ⓐ Ⓑ Ⓒ Ⓓ

REFERENCE SHEET

Directions

For each question from 1 to 18, solve each problem, choose the best answer from the choices provided, and fill in the corresponding bubble on your answer sheet.

For questions 19 and 22, solve the problem and enter your answer in the grid on the answer sheet.

Refer to the directions before question 19 for how to enter your answers in the grid. You may use any available space for scratch work.

REFERENCE

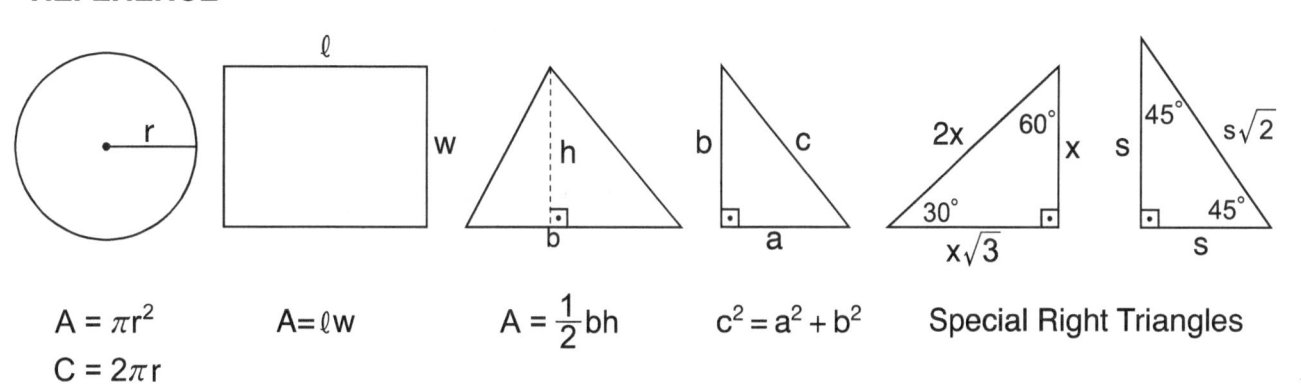

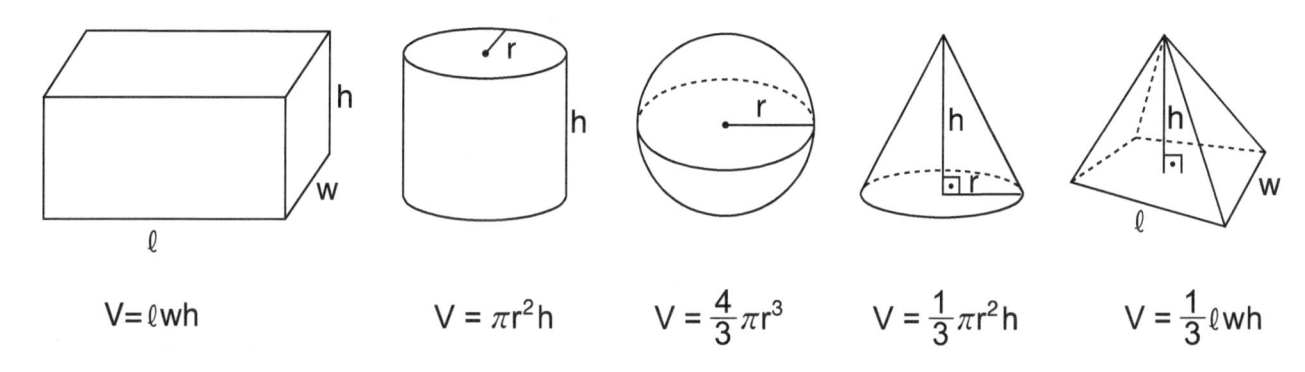

$A = \pi r^2$
$C = 2\pi r$

$A = \ell w$

$A = \frac{1}{2}bh$

$c^2 = a^2 + b^2$

Special Right Triangles

$V = \ell wh$

$V = \pi r^2 h$

$V = \frac{4}{3}\pi r^3$

$V = \frac{1}{3}\pi r^2 h$

$V = \frac{1}{3}\ell wh$

The number of degrees in a circle is 360.

The number of radians in a circle is 2π.

The sum of the measures in degrees of the angles of a triangle is 180.

MATH PRACTICE TEST IV
35 Minutes - 22 Questions
MODULE II

1. Suppose that x is an integer such that $\frac{x}{4}$ is 10 greater than $\frac{x}{5}$. Which of the following is the value of x?

A) 180

B) 190

C) 200

D) 210

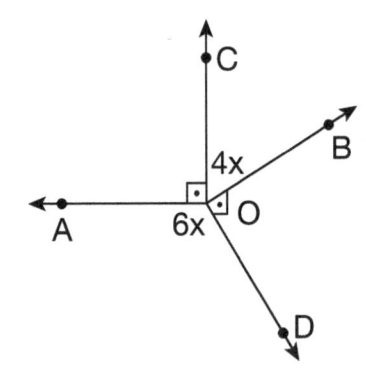

2.

From the figure $\angle(BOC)=4x$, and $\angle(AOD)=6x$. What is the value of x?

A) 12°

B) 16°

C) 18°

D) 20°

3. What are the solutions of x in the following system of equations?

$$x^2 - 4x + y = 14$$
$$5x - y = 6$$

A) (−1, 4)

B) (4, 5)

C) (−4, −5)

D) (−5, 4)

4. What is the solution(s) for y in the following equation?

$$\frac{12}{\sqrt[5]{y}} = 6$$

A) 16 and −16

B) 32 and −32

C) 16 only

D) 32 only

5. $$f(x) = \begin{cases} -2x+3, & x<0 \\ x^2+4, & x\geq 0 \end{cases}$$

From the above function, find $f(1) + f(-2)$?

A) 7

B) 8

C) 9

D) 12

MATH PRACTICE TEST IV
35 Minutes - 22 Questions
MODULE II

6. In the following cylinder shape, if the volume of the cylinder 72π cm³, find the radius of the cylinder.

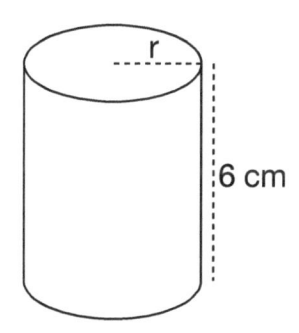

[cylinder with radius r and height 6 cm]

A) $\sqrt{3}$ cm

B) $2\sqrt{3}$ cm

C) $3\sqrt{3}$ cm

D) 6 cm

7. If a is the average of 8k and 10, b is the average of 6k and 10, and c is the average of 10k and 40, what is the average of a, b, and c in terms of k?

A) $4k + 20$

B) $4k - 15$

C) $4k + 15$

D) $4k + 10$

8. Two classes took a science test. The first class had 20 students and their average test score was 90%. The second class had 24 students and their average score was 85%. If the teacher combined the test scores of both classes, what is the average of both classes together? Round your answer to the nearest percent.

A) 82%

B) 83%

C) 86%

D) 87%

9. Formula A: $A = \dfrac{3x+y}{7}$

Formula B: $A = \dfrac{2x+5y}{12}$

Base on the formulas, what is the value of x in terms of y?

A) $x = \dfrac{23}{22}y$

B) $x = \dfrac{22}{23}y$

C) $x = 23y$

D) $x = 22y$

10. If $\dfrac{x}{4} = 7$ and $x + y = 35$, what is the value of $x - y$?

A) 18

B) 21

C) 24

D) 27

93

MATH PRACTICE TEST IV
35 Minutes - 22 Questions
MODULE II

11. The athlete moves from A to B and the distance is $\frac{1}{4}$ of the total. When the athlete arrives at C, the distance equals to $\frac{1}{3}$ of the total. When the athlete arrives at B, the time is 8:50AM. When the athlete arrives at C, the time is 9:00AM. What time is it when the athlete arrives to D?

A) 10:00 A.M.

B) 10:20 A.M.

C) 9:40 A.M.

D) 9:50 A.M.

12. If a,b and c are positive integers and;

a + b is odd

a · c is even

b · c is odd

Which one of the following is must be an odd number?

A) a^2b

B) a + 2b

C) b^3c

D) a + 2c

13. $\frac{7\sin x° + 2\cos x°}{4\cos x° + 5\sin x°} = \frac{3}{5}$, then what is cot x°?

A) 7

B) 9

C) 10

D) 11

14. $\frac{|x-y|}{|y-z|} = 6$

From the above equation, if x = 18 and y = 6, then which of the following could be the value of z?

A) 3

B) 6

C) 8

D) 9

MATH PRACTICE TEST IV
35 Minutes - 22 Questions
MODULE II

15.

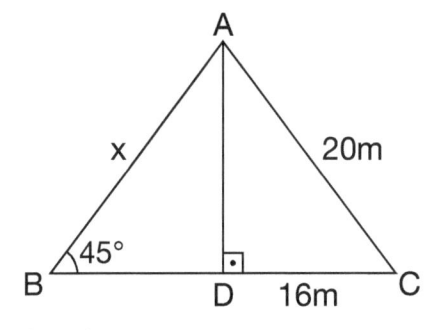

|AC| = 20m
|DC| = 16m
m(A͡BD) = 45°

What is the length of x?

A) 8m

B) $8\sqrt{2}$ m

C) $12\sqrt{2}$ m

D) 16m

16.

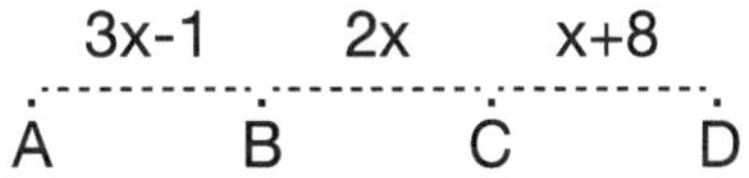

```
    3x-1    2x    x+8
 ·-------·-----·-----·
 A       B     C     D
```

Note: Figure not drawn to scale.

On |AD| above, and |AB| = 2|CD|.

|AB| = 3x − 1

|BC| = 2x

|CD| = x + 8

What is the length of |AD|?

A) 103

B) 105

C) 107

D) 109

17. In the xy−plane the point (3, 8) lies on the graph of the function f.

$f(x) = t - 3x^2$, Where t is a constant. What is the value of t?

A) 31

B) 33

C) 35

D) 37

18. $\boxed{X} \xrightarrow{-5} \boxed{} \xrightarrow{\div 3} \boxed{} \xrightarrow{+10} \boxed{} \xrightarrow{\times 2} \boxed{50}$

According to the figure above, what is x?

A) 50

B) 40

C) 30

D) 20

MATH PRACTICE TEST IV
35 Minutes - 22 Questions
MODULE II

19. If the ratio of the circumference to the area of a circle is 2 to 3, what is the radius of the circle?

20. $2^x \cdot 2^x \cdot 2^x \cdot 2^x = 64^2$, then find x.

21. $3^y + 3^y + 3^y = 81^2$, then find y.

22. If $x = 7y$ and $\dfrac{x}{2} - \dfrac{y}{3} = 57$, then find x.

PRACTICE TEST IV ANSWER SHEET
MODULE II

1. Ⓐ Ⓑ Ⓒ Ⓓ
2. Ⓐ Ⓑ Ⓒ Ⓓ
3. Ⓐ Ⓑ Ⓒ Ⓓ
4. Ⓐ Ⓑ Ⓒ Ⓓ
5. Ⓐ Ⓑ Ⓒ Ⓓ
6. Ⓐ Ⓑ Ⓒ Ⓓ
7. Ⓐ Ⓑ Ⓒ Ⓓ
8. Ⓐ Ⓑ Ⓒ Ⓓ
9. Ⓐ Ⓑ Ⓒ Ⓓ
10. Ⓐ Ⓑ Ⓒ Ⓓ
11. Ⓐ Ⓑ Ⓒ Ⓓ
12. Ⓐ Ⓑ Ⓒ Ⓓ
13. Ⓐ Ⓑ Ⓒ Ⓓ
14. Ⓐ Ⓑ Ⓒ Ⓓ
15. Ⓐ Ⓑ Ⓒ Ⓓ
16. Ⓐ Ⓑ Ⓒ Ⓓ
17. Ⓐ Ⓑ Ⓒ Ⓓ
18. Ⓐ Ⓑ Ⓒ Ⓓ

19.
20.
21.
22.

PRACTICE TEST IV
MODULE I ANSWER KEY

1)	B
2)	C
3)	D
4)	A
5)	A
6)	B
7)	A
8)	A
9)	B
10)	C
11)	B
12)	D
13)	C
14)	B
15)	B
16)	D
17)	A
18)	254
19)	12
20)	28
21)	12%
22)	16/3

PRACTICE TEST IV
MODULE I SOLUTIONS

1. $x^{\frac{1}{3}} = 64$, then $x^{\frac{1}{3}} = 4^3$ ⟶ multily each power by 3 to find x

$$x^{\frac{1(3)}{3}} = 4^{3(3)}$$

$$x = 4^9$$

$$\frac{x}{2} = \frac{4^9}{2^1} = \frac{(2^2)^9}{2^1} = \frac{2^{18}}{2^1} = 2^{18-1} = 2^{17}$$

Correct Answer : B

2. $9^{2x-3} = 27^{3x-7}$

$(3^2)^{2x-3} = (3^3)^{3x-7}$ ⟶ use power to power rule.

$(3)^{4x-6} = (3)^{9x-21}$ ⟶ since base are same power must be equal.

$4x - 6 = 9x - 21$ ⟶ simplify

$21 - 6 = 9x - 4x$

$15 = 5x$

$3 = x$

Correct Answer : C

3. $\frac{x-6}{3} = \frac{2x-7}{4}$ (cross multiply)

$4(x - 6) = 3(2x - 7)$

$4x - 24 = 6x - 21$ (simplify)

$-24 + 21 = 6x - 4x$

$-3 = 2x$

$-\frac{3}{2} = x$

Correct Answer : D

4. $3y - \frac{x}{4} = 10$

$3y - 10 = \frac{x}{4}$ ⟶ multiply both sides by 2.

$2(3y - 10) = \frac{x}{4}(2)$

$6y - 20 = \frac{x}{2}$

Correct Answer : A

5. $\frac{4}{1+i\sqrt{3}} = \frac{4}{1+i\sqrt{3}}\left(\frac{1-i\sqrt{3}}{1-i\sqrt{3}}\right)$

$= \frac{4-4i\sqrt{3}}{1-3i^2} = \frac{4-4i\sqrt{3}}{1+3}$

$= \frac{4-4i\sqrt{3}}{4} = 1 - i\sqrt{3}$

$i^2 = -1$

Correct Answer : A

6. $\frac{1}{a-b} + \frac{1}{a+b} = \frac{2}{9}$

$= \frac{1}{a-b}\left(\frac{a+b}{a+b}\right) + \frac{1}{a+b}\left(\frac{a-b}{a+b}\right) = \frac{2}{9}$

$\frac{a+b+a-b}{a^2-b^2} = \frac{2}{9}$

$\frac{2a}{36} = \frac{2}{9}$

$18a = 72$

$a = 4$

Correct Answer : B

99

PRACTICE TEST IV
MODULE I SOLUTIONS

7. Tricio: $6\frac{3}{4} = \frac{27}{4}$

Laurie: $6\frac{1}{2} = \frac{13}{2}$

Jim: $6\frac{1}{4} = \frac{25}{4}$ ⟩ Laurie and Mark

Mark: $6\frac{1}{2} = \frac{13}{2}$

Correct Answer : A

8. $|\sqrt{5} - \sqrt{6}| + |3 - \sqrt{6}| + |\sqrt{20} - 3| =$

$-\sqrt{5} + \sqrt{6} + 3 - \sqrt{6} + \sqrt{20} - 3 = \sqrt{5}$

Correct Answer : A

9. First plan: $23 membership fee and $7 per visit ⟶ convert to the equation.

y = $23 + 7x

Second plan: only per visit fee of $13 ⟶ convert to the equation.

y = 13x (no membership fee)

Correct Answer : B

10. The inverse of an operation is gets you back to the number you started with.

$14 \cdot 7 = 98$

$\frac{98}{2} = 49$

$49 + 5 = 54$

$\frac{54}{6} = 9$

A = 9 and 9 is a perfect square so option C is true for A.

Correct Answer : C

11. $y = x^2 + 9$ ⟩ Use substation method to find x.
$y = 7x - 3$

$x^2 + 9 = 7x - 3$

$x^2 - 7x + 12 = 0$

$(x - 3)(x - 4) = 0$

$x = 3$ or $x = 4$

Correct Answer : B

12. $\frac{k}{2km} = \frac{1}{k+m}$ (Cross multiply)

$k(k + m) = 2km$

$k^2 + km = 2km$

$k^2 = km$

$k = m$

Correct Answer : D

PRACTICE TEST IV
MODULE I SOLUTIONS

13. If x hour is equivalent to y minutes:

$x = 60y$

Correct Answer : C

14. $(x-h)^2 + (y-k)^2 = r^2$

$(x-3)^2 + (y+7)^2 = 16$

$r^2 = 16$

$r = 4$

Correct Answer : B

15.

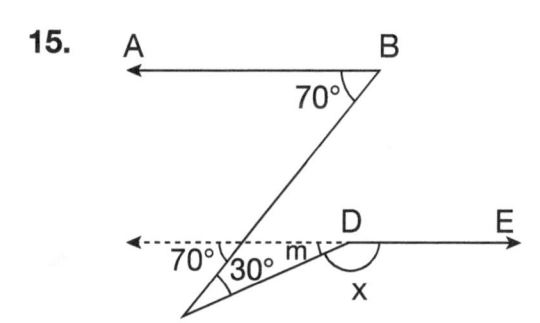

Since AB // DE

$m + 30° = 70°$ $m = 40°$

$m + x = 180°$

$40° + x = 180°$ $x = 140°$

Correct Answer : B

16. If $x^3 \cdot y^2 > 0$ so y^2 is always positive then $x > 0$

If $x^2 \cdot z > 0$ so x^2 is always positive then $z > 0$

If $y^3 \cdot z < 0$ so we knows $z > 0$ then $y < 0$

Correct Answer : D

17.

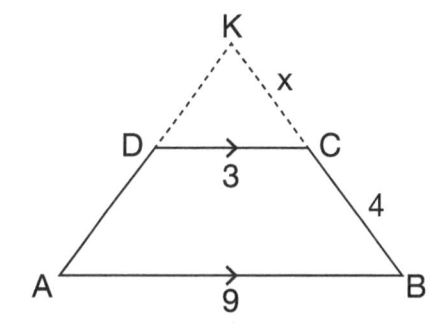

From similarity theorem

$\dfrac{x}{x+4} = \dfrac{3}{9}$ $\dfrac{x}{x+4} = \dfrac{1}{3}$ (cross multiply)

$3x = x + 4$

$3x - x = 4$

$2x = 4$

$x = 2$

Correct Answer : A

18. since x and y are positive integers:

$\sqrt{x} = y^4 = 16$, then

$\sqrt{x} = 16$, $x = 256$

$y^4 = 16$,

$y^4 = 2^4$

$y = 2$

$x - y = 256 - 2 = 254$

Correct Answer : 254

PRACTICE TEST IV
MODULE I SOLUTIONS

19. Line that passes through $(-7, 3)$ and $(2,k)$ has a slope of 1.

Slope $= \dfrac{y_2 - y_1}{x_2 - x_1} = \dfrac{k-3}{2-(-7)}$

$\dfrac{k-3}{9} = 1$

$k - 3 = 9$

$k = 12$

Correct Answer : 12

20. $\dfrac{1}{2}x + y = 18$ (multiply all equations by -2.)

$-x - 2y = -36$

$x - \dfrac{3}{2}y = 8$

$+$ ―――――――

$-\dfrac{7}{2}y = -28$

$y = 8$

plug in y in one of the above equations and then find x.

$\dfrac{1}{2}x + y = 18$

$\dfrac{1}{2}x + 8 = 18$

$\dfrac{1}{2}x = 18 - 8$

$\dfrac{1}{2}x = 10$

$x = 20$

$x + y = 8 + 20$

$= 28$

Correct Answer : 28

21. Decrease: $\dfrac{\text{decrease amount}}{\text{original amount}} = \dfrac{\$125 - \$110}{\$125}$

$= \dfrac{15}{125} = \dfrac{3}{25}$

$= \dfrac{3}{25} \times \dfrac{4}{4} = \dfrac{12}{100} = 12\%$

Correct Answer : 12%

22. $k - 9 + \dfrac{5k}{2} = \dfrac{1}{2}k + 7$

$\dfrac{7k}{2} - 9 = \dfrac{1}{2}k + 7$

$\dfrac{7k}{2} - \dfrac{1}{2}k = 7 + 9$

$\dfrac{6k}{2} = 16$

$3k = 16$

$k = \dfrac{16}{3}$

Correct Answer : $\dfrac{16}{3}$

102

PRACTICE TEST IV
MODULE II ANSWER KEY

1)	C
2)	C
3)	D
4)	D
5)	D
6)	B
7)	D
8)	D
9)	A
10)	B
11)	B

12)	C
13)	C
14)	C
15)	C
16)	D
17)	C
18)	A
19)	3
20)	3
21)	7
22)	Y = 18

PRACTICE TEST IV
MODULE II SOLUTIONS

1. $\frac{x}{4} = \frac{x}{5} + 10$

$\frac{x}{4} - \frac{x}{5}$ (Find LCD of both numbers)

$\frac{5x}{20} - \frac{4x}{20} = 10$

$\frac{x}{20} = 10$

$x = 200$

Correct Answer : C

2. $6x + 4x + 90° + 90° = 360°$

$10x = 360° - 180°$

$10x = 180°$

$x = 18°$

Correct Answer : C

3. $x^2 - 4x + y = 14$ and $5x - y = 6$, then $y = 5x - 6$

$x^2 - 4x + 5x - 6 = 14$

$x^2 + x - 20 = 0$

$(x + 5)(x - 4) = 0$

$x = -5$ or $x = 4$

$x = (-5, 4)$

Correct Answer : D

4. $\frac{12}{\sqrt[5]{y}} = 6$

$\sqrt[5]{y} = \frac{12}{6}$

$\sqrt[5]{y} = 2$, $\sqrt[5]{y^5} = 2^5$

$y = 2^5 = 32$

Correct Answer : D

5. $f(x) = x^2 + 4$, when $x \geq 0$

$f(1) = 1^2 + 4 = 5$

$f(x) = -x + 5$, when $x < 0$

$f(-2) = -(-2) + 5 = 2 + 5 = 7$

$f(1) + f(-2) = 5 + 7 = 12$

Correct Answer : D

6.

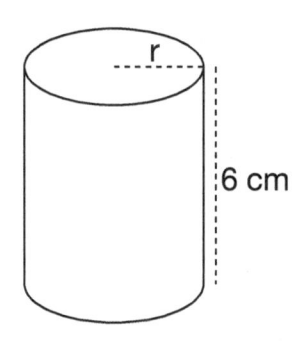

Volume of cylinder $= \pi r^2 h$

$\pi r^2 \cdot 6cm = 72\pi cm^3$

$r^2 \cdot 6cm = 72 cm^3$

$r^2 = \frac{72 cm^3}{6cm}$, $r^2 = 12 cm^2$

$r = 2\sqrt{3} cm$

Correct Answer : B

PRACTICE TEST IV
MODULE II SOLUTIONS

7. $a = \dfrac{8k+10}{2} = 4k+5$

$b = \dfrac{6k+10}{2} = 3k+5$

$c = \dfrac{10k+40}{2} = 5k+20$

Average of a, b, and c $= \dfrac{a+b+c}{3}$

$= \dfrac{4k+5+3k+5+5k+20}{3}$

$= \dfrac{12k+30}{3} = 4k+15$

Correct Answer : D

8. $x = \dfrac{20(0.90) + 24(0.85)}{44}$

$x = \dfrac{18 + 20.4}{44}$

$x = \dfrac{38.4}{44}$

$x \approx 87\%$

Correct Answer : D

9. Formula A = Formula B

$\dfrac{3x+y}{7} = \dfrac{2x+5y}{12}$ (Cross Multiply)

$36x + 12y = 14x + 35y$

$36x - 14x = 35y - 12y$

$22x = 23y$

$x = \dfrac{23}{22}y$

Correct Answer : A

10. $\dfrac{x}{4} = 7$, $x = 28$

$28 + y = 35$

$y = 35 - 28$

$y = 7$

$x - y = 28 - 7 = 21$

Correct Answer : B

11. Let Distance $|AD| = 12x$

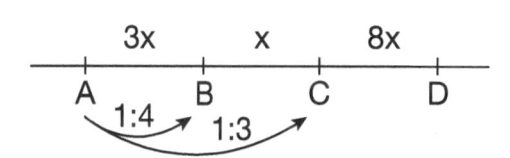

so $|AB| = 3x$

$|AC| = 4x$

$|CD| = 8x$

$|BC| = x$

When the athlete arrive from B to C since diffrence between the time is 10 minutes.

x distance 10 minutes

8x distance 80 minutes

9:00 a.m + 80 minutes = 10:20 A.M

Correct Answer : B

12. If b · c is odd then b and c have to be odd. Then if a · c is even and we know c is odd so a has to be even. Thus a^2b, $a + 2b$, and $a + 2c$ is even but b^3c is odd.

Correct Answer : C

105

PRACTICE TEST IV
MODULE II SOLUTIONS

13. $35\sin x° + 10\cos x° = 12\cos x° + 15\sin x°$

$20\sin x° = 2\cos x°$

$10\sin x° = \cos x°$

$10 = \dfrac{\cos x°}{\sin x°}$

$\cot x° = \dfrac{\cos x°}{\sin x°} = 10$

Correct Answer : C

14. $\dfrac{|x-y|}{|y-z|} = 6$

If $x = 18$ and $y = 6$, then plug in equation.

$\dfrac{|18-6|}{|6-z|} = 6$

$\dfrac{|12|}{|6-z|} = 6$, $\dfrac{12}{|6-z|} = 6$

$|6-z| = 2$

$6-z = \pm 2$

$6 \pm 2 = z$

$6+2 = z$ or $6-2 = z$

$8 = z$ or $4 = z$

Correct Answer : C

15. $|AD|^2 + 16^2 = 20^2$

$|AD| = 12m$

$s(\widehat{BAC}) = 45°$, then $|BD| = 12m$

$|AB| = x = 12\sqrt{2}\,m$

Correct Answer : C

16. $|AB| = 2|CD|$, then $3x - 1 = 2(x+8)$

$3x - 1 = 2x + 16 \longrightarrow x = 17$

$|AD| = 3x - 1 + 2x + x + 8$

$|AD| = 6x + 7 \longrightarrow |AD| = 6 \cdot 17 + 7 = 109$

Correct Answer : D

17. We know $x = 3$ and $y = 8$, then $f(x) = t - 3x^2$

$f(3) = t - 3 \cdot (3)^2$

$8 = t - 27$

$t = 35$

Correct Answer : C

18. Starting from back then;

$50 \div 2 = 25$

$25 - 10 = 15$

$15 \cdot 3 = 45$

$45 + 5 = 50$, then x is 50.

Correct Answer : A

PRACTICE TEST IV
MODULE II SOLUTIONS

19. $\dfrac{\text{ratio of circumference}}{\text{ratio of arc}} = \dfrac{2\pi r}{\pi r^2}$

$= \dfrac{2\pi r}{\pi r^2} = \dfrac{2}{3}$

$\dfrac{2\cancel{r}}{\cancel{r}^2} = \dfrac{2}{3}$

$\dfrac{2}{r} = \dfrac{2}{3} \quad r = 3$

Correct Answer : 3

20. $2^x \cdot 2^x \cdot 2^x \cdot 2^x = 64^2 \longrightarrow$ Use exponent multiply rule.

$2^{x+x+x+x} = (2^6)^2$

$2^{4x} = 2^{12} \longrightarrow 4x = 12, \ x = 3$

Correct Answer : 3

21. $3^y + 3^y + 3^y = 81^2$

$3^y(1+1+1) = 81^2$

$3^y \cdot 3^1 = (3^4)^2$

$3^{y+1} = 3^8$

$y + 1 = 8, \ y = 7$

Correct Answer : 7

22. If $x = 7y$ and $\dfrac{x}{2} - \dfrac{y}{3} = 57$,

$\dfrac{7y}{2} - \dfrac{y}{3} = 57 \text{ (find LCD)}$

$\dfrac{21y}{6} - \dfrac{2y}{6} = 57 \text{ (cross multiply)}$

$21y - 2y = 6 \cdot 57$

$19y = 342$

$y = 18$

Correct Answer : 18

107

REFERENCE SHEET

Directions

For each question from 1–17, solve each problem, choose the best answer from the choices provided, and fill in the corresponding bubble on your answer sheet.

For questions 18 to 22, solve the problem and enter your answer in the grid on the answer sheet.

Refer to the directions before question 18 for how to enter your answers in the grid. You may use any available space for scratch work.

REFERENCE

$A = \pi r^2$
$C = 2\pi r$

$A = \ell w$

$A = \frac{1}{2}bh$

$c^2 = a^2 + b^2$

Special Right Triangles

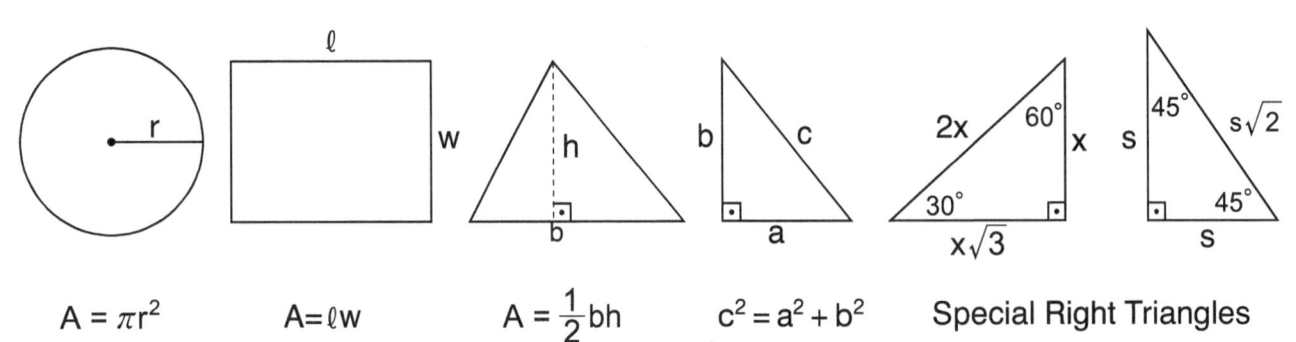

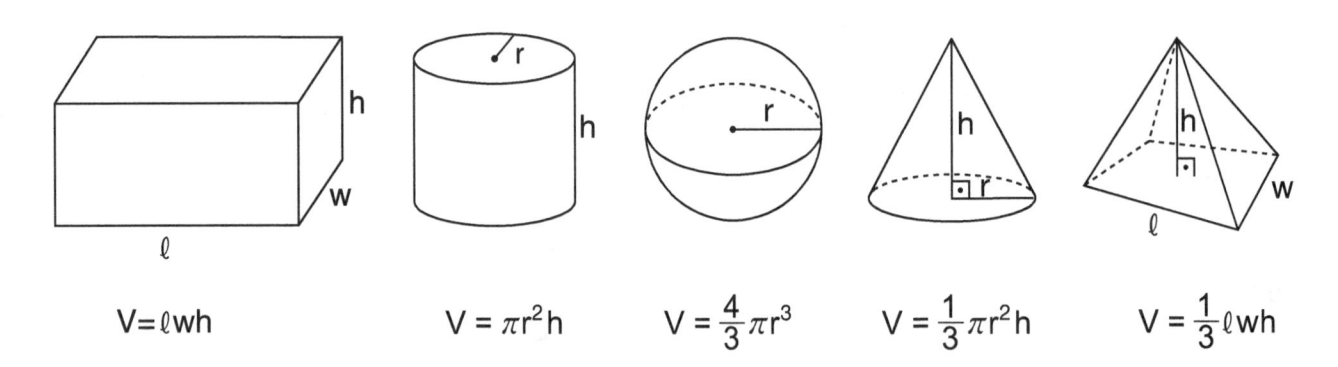

$V = \ell w h$

$V = \pi r^2 h$

$V = \frac{4}{3}\pi r^3$

$V = \frac{1}{3}\pi r^2 h$

$V = \frac{1}{3}\ell w h$

The number of degrees in a circle is 360.

The number of radians in a circle is 2π.

The sum of the measures in degrees of the angles of a triangle is 180.

MATH PRACTICE TEST V
35 Minutes - 22 Questions
MODULE I

1.

I.

II.

III.

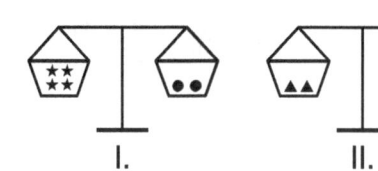

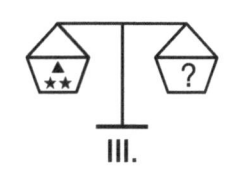

According to the diagram, which group of weights from figures I and II are equal to the weight of the question mark?

A) ● ● ●

B) ● ●

C) ● ● ▲

D) ● ● ★

2. Simplify $\dfrac{x^2y + xy^2 - xy}{x^2 + xy - x}$

A) x

B) y

C) 2xy

D) −x

3. The tree grows everyday at $\sqrt{x}$ cm.

60cm after 5th day, 72cm after 9th day

What is the height of the tree after the 15th day?

A) 80cm

B) 90cm

C) 100cm

D) 120cm

4. $\dfrac{x+3}{4} - \dfrac{x}{3} = \dfrac{3}{2}$, find the value of x.

A) −3

B) −6

C) −9

D) −12

5. If y varies inversely as x and x = 8 when y = 6, find y when x = 10.

A) 2.8

B) 3.8

C) 4.8

D) 5.8

109

MATH PRACTICE TEST V
35 Minutes - 22 Questions
MODULE I

6. $\sqrt[2]{x+16} + \sqrt[2]{x} = 8$, then x can be which of the following?

A) 3

B) 5

C) 7

D) 9

7. How many solutions does the system of equations shown below have?

$$2x = y + 4$$
$$4x - 5y = 8$$

A) Zero

B) 1

C) 2

D) Many/infinity

8. Simplify $\sqrt{27} - \sqrt{81} + \sqrt{243}$.

A) $3\sqrt{3} - 9$

B) $6\sqrt{3} - 9$

C) $9\sqrt{3} - 9$

D) $12\sqrt{3} - 9$

9. If $a = \sqrt{3}$ and $b = \sqrt{2}$ then find $\dfrac{a}{b} - \dfrac{b}{a}$.

A) $\dfrac{\sqrt{6}}{6}$

B) $\dfrac{1}{\sqrt{5}}$

C) $\dfrac{1}{\sqrt{3}}$

D) $\dfrac{1}{\sqrt{2}}$

10. The function $f(x) = (x - 3)(x - 5)(x + 8)$ will intersect the x-axis how many times?

A) 0

B) 1

C) 2

D) 3

11. If x is a positive integer and $x^2 + x - 12 = 0$, what is the value of $x + 3$?

A) 3

B) 6

C) 9

D) 12

110

MATH PRACTICE TEST V
35 Minutes - 22 Questions
MODULE I

12. In a right triangle, the cosine of angle B is $\frac{3}{5}$ and the sine of angle B is $\frac{4}{5}$.

What is the ratio of the longest side to the shortest side?

A) $\frac{4}{3}$

B) $\frac{4}{5}$

C) $\frac{3}{4}$

D) $\frac{5}{3}$

13. Suppose that x is an integer such that $\frac{x}{3}$ is 6 greater than $\frac{x}{4}$. Which of the following is the value of x?

A) 24

B) 36

C) 72

D) 96

14. Mr. Johnson gave the following list of numbers to his class. He asked the class to find all of the composite numbers in the list.

3, 4, 7, 11, 14, 19, 21, 33

Which of these shows all of the composite numbers in the list?

A) 3, 7, 11, 19

B) 4, 14, 21, 33

C) 4, 19, 21, 33

D) 4, 11, 21, 33

15.

x x y   z z y   y y z

1st basket   2nd basket   3rd basket

There are three baskets given above, and they have three kinds of squares.

The sequence of the weight of baskets is $1^{st} > 2^{nd} > 3^{rd}$. Which of the following statement is true?

(x = x's weight, y = y's weight, z = z's weight)

A) x > y > z

B) x > z > y

C) y > x > z

D) y > z > x

111

MATH PRACTICE TEST V
35 Minutes - 22 Questions
MODULE I

16.
$$x = \$7 + 5k$$
$$y = \$5.5 + 10k$$

In above equation, x represents the price in dollars of apple juice and y represents the price in dollars of orange juice at the farmer's market and k is the same amount per week. What is the price of apple juice when it's the same as the price of orange juice?

A) $5

B) $6

C) $6.5

D) $8.5

17. The linear function g (x) is shown in the table below. Which of following defines g (x)?

x	g(x)
1	15
2	17
3	19

A) 2x + 10

B) 2x + 13

C) 2x − 13

D) 2x + 5

18. If 4a + 5b = 16 and a = 3 then find b?

MATH PRACTICE TEST V
35 Minutes - 22 Questions
MODULE I

19. If 6 is one of the solutions of the equation $x^2 - 3ax - 24 = 0$, what is the value of a?

20. For the function below, m>0 is a constant and f(2)=20. What is the value of f(5)?

$$f(x) = mx^2 - 4$$

21. In the following circle, O is the center of circle. What is the value of x?

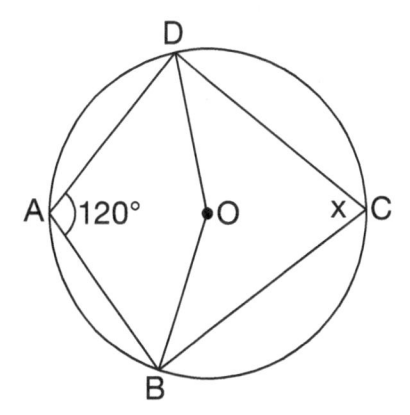

22. If the following polynomial P(x) is divisible by x+1 then find the remainder.

$$P(x) = x^{2018} + x^{2019} + x^{2020}$$

PRACTICE TEST V ANSWER SHEET
MODULE I

1. Ⓐ Ⓑ Ⓒ Ⓓ
2. Ⓐ Ⓑ Ⓒ Ⓓ
3. Ⓐ Ⓑ Ⓒ Ⓓ
4. Ⓐ Ⓑ Ⓒ Ⓓ
5. Ⓐ Ⓑ Ⓒ Ⓓ
6. Ⓐ Ⓑ Ⓒ Ⓓ
7. Ⓐ Ⓑ Ⓒ Ⓓ
8. Ⓐ Ⓑ Ⓒ Ⓓ
9. Ⓐ Ⓑ Ⓒ Ⓓ
10. Ⓐ Ⓑ Ⓒ Ⓓ
11. Ⓐ Ⓑ Ⓒ Ⓓ
12. Ⓐ Ⓑ Ⓒ Ⓓ
13. Ⓐ Ⓑ Ⓒ Ⓓ
14. Ⓐ Ⓑ Ⓒ Ⓓ
15. Ⓐ Ⓑ Ⓒ Ⓓ
16. Ⓐ Ⓑ Ⓒ Ⓓ
17. Ⓐ Ⓑ Ⓒ Ⓓ

REFERENCE SHEET

Directions

For each question from 1 to 18, solve each problem, choose the best answer from the choices provided, and fill in the corresponding bubble on your answer sheet.

For questions 19 and 22, solve the problem and enter your answer in the grid on the answer sheet.

Refer to the directions before question 19 for how to enter your answers in the grid. You may use any available space for scratch work.

REFERENCE

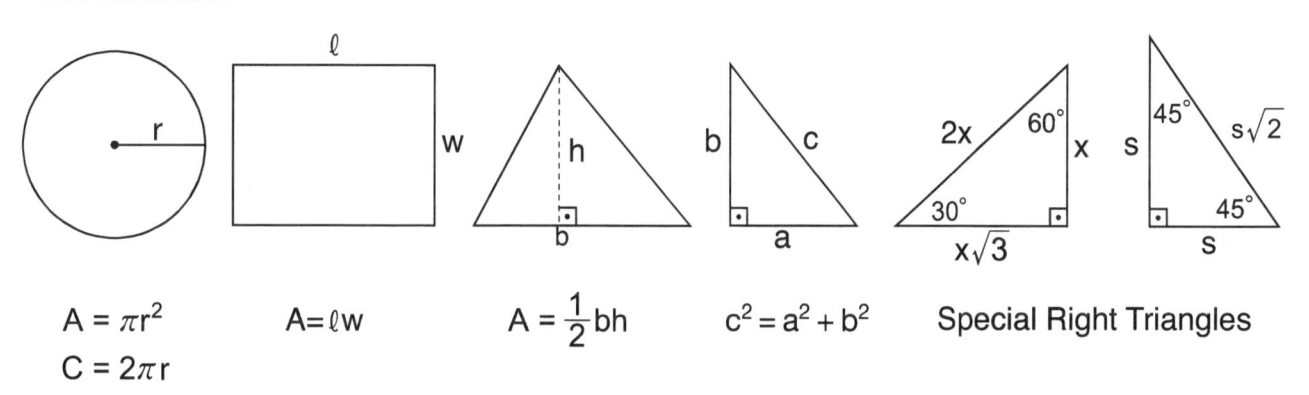

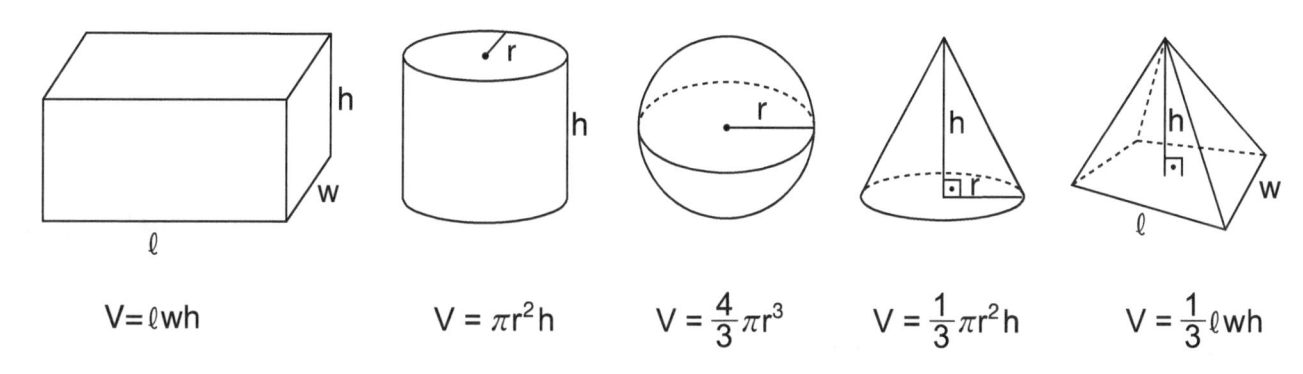

$A = \pi r^2$
$C = 2\pi r$

$A = \ell w$

$A = \frac{1}{2} bh$

$c^2 = a^2 + b^2$

Special Right Triangles

$V = \ell wh$

$V = \pi r^2 h$

$V = \frac{4}{3}\pi r^3$

$V = \frac{1}{3}\pi r^2 h$

$V = \frac{1}{3}\ell wh$

The number of degrees in a circle is 360.

The number of radians in a circle is 2π.

The sum of the measures in degrees of the angles of a triangle is 180.

MATH PRACTICE TEST V
35 Minutes - 22 Questions
MODULE II

1. What are the zeros of the function $f(x) = x^3 + 6x^2 + 9x$?

A) 0, 2

B) 0, −2

C) 0, 3

D) 0, −3

2. If x is a positive real number and $x - 2\sqrt{x} - 3 = 0$ then find $\dfrac{x}{x-1}$

A) $\dfrac{1}{2}$

B) $\dfrac{1}{4}$

C) $\dfrac{9}{8}$

D) $\dfrac{5}{3}$

3. The sum of five consecutive positive integers is 75. What is the greatest possible value of one of these integers?

A) 13

B) 15

C) 17

D) 27

4. If the ratio of $\dfrac{1}{3} : \dfrac{1}{b}$ is equal to $\dfrac{1}{18} : \dfrac{1}{12}$, what is the value of b?

A) 9

B) $\dfrac{9}{2}$

C) $\dfrac{2}{9}$

D) 2

5. If $3^{2x-4} = 27^{x-6}$, then what is the value of x?

A) 12

B) 14

C) 16

D) 18

6. For a > 5, which of the following is equivalent to

$$\dfrac{1}{\dfrac{1}{x+3}+\dfrac{1}{x+5}} = ?$$

A) $\dfrac{2x+8}{x^2+8x+15}$

B) $\dfrac{x^2+8x+15}{2x+8x}$

C) $\dfrac{2x+8}{x^2-8x+15}$

D) $x^2+8x+15$

116

MATH PRACTICE TEST V
35 Minutes - 22 Questions
MODULE II

7. Which of the following complex number is equivalent to $\left(\dfrac{1+i}{1-i}\right)^{2020}$?

A) 1

B) −1

C) i

D) −i

8. The following chart show market stock in supermarkets which buy tea, coffee, soda and water after they sell them. Their prices are given in the chart.

	Cost	Sale
Tea	20	25
Coffee	12	18
Soda	20	24
Water	90	120

Which product has the highest rate of profit?

A) Tea

B) Coffee

C) Soda

D) Water

9. Φ and ⊕ are functions on real numbers.

$$x\Phi y = \dfrac{x^2+y}{4} \text{ and } x \oplus y = \dfrac{3xy}{5}$$

$(2\Phi 1) \oplus (3\Phi 1) = ?$

A) $\dfrac{25}{4}$

B) $\dfrac{27}{4}$

C) $\dfrac{15}{8}$

D) $\dfrac{17}{2}$

10.

a   b   c

I.   II.   III.

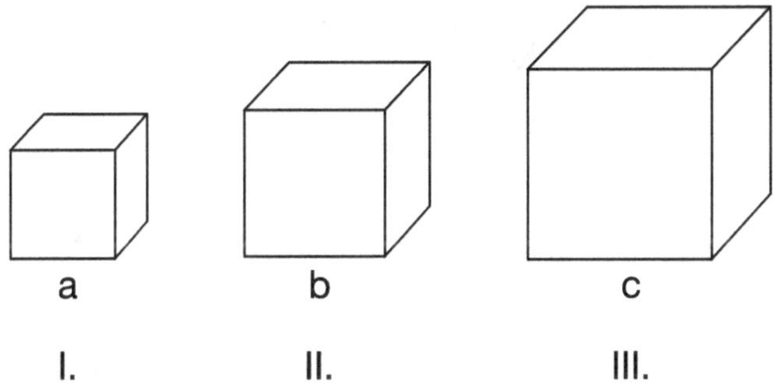

There are three cubes given above. Their side length is given under the cubes.
'I' is a, 'II' is b, 'III' is c. Their volumes are V_a, V_b, and V_c.

$$c = 2b = 3a$$

$\dfrac{1}{V_a} + \dfrac{1}{V_b} + \dfrac{1}{V_c} = \dfrac{1}{6}$, then find volume of V_c = ?

A) 216

B) 125

C) 64

D) 27

MATH PRACTICE TEST V
35 Minutes - 22 Questions
MODULE II

11. The table below shows the results of a survey on how students get to school. A circle graph is to be used to display the data. What percent of the graph represents the car transportation?

Number of Students	Transportation
90	School bus
60	Car
10	Walk
40	Bike

A) 30%

B) 35%

C) 40%

D) 45%

12. If $2^{4a} = \dfrac{32}{2^a}$, then find the value of a.

A) 0

B) 1

C) 2

D) 3

13. $x \triangle y = \begin{cases} y^2 - x \, , \, x \leq y \\ \dfrac{-y}{3} \, , \, x > y \end{cases}$

What is the solution of $(-4) \triangle \left[\dfrac{1}{4} \triangle (-3)\right] = ?$

A) 2

B) 3

C) 4

D) 5

14. Which of following could be a value of k in the following equation?

$$2k^2 - 3k + 1 = 0$$

A) 0

B) 1

C) 2

D) 3

15. On the xy coordinate grid, a line K contains the points (2, 3) and (−2, 7). If the line K is perpendicular to L at (3, 1), which of following is the equation of the line L?

A) y = x − 2

B) y = −x + 4

C) y = x + 4

D) y = 2x − 4

118

MATH PRACTICE TEST V
35 Minutes - 22 Questions
MODULE II

16. What is the solution of the following system of equations?

$$3y = 6 + 4x$$
$$y = 8 - 2x$$

A) (1, 4)

B) (1.8, 4.4)

C) (2, 4)

D) (−1.8, 4)

17. If $6x = 8y + 10$ and $x - 3y = -5$ then what is the value of $\frac{y}{2}$?

A) 2

B) 3

C) 4

D) 6

18. What is the one possible value of x−y?

$$\frac{6}{8} < \frac{x}{2} - \frac{2y}{4} < \frac{3}{2}$$

A) 1

B) 2

C) 3

D) 4

19. $\frac{2a-3}{a-2} - 4 = \frac{3}{a-2}$, find the value of a

20. If $x^2 + 2x - 15 = (x - a)(x + b)$ for all values of x, what is the value of a · b?

21. If $x^2 + 12x - 13 = 0$ and $x > 0$, what is the value of $x + 10$?

22. $6x - ay + 12 = 0$, if the slope of the equation is $\frac{1}{3}$, what is the value of a?

119

PRACTICE TEST V ANSWER SHEET
MODULE II

1. Ⓐ Ⓑ Ⓒ Ⓓ   7. Ⓐ Ⓑ Ⓒ Ⓓ   13. Ⓐ Ⓑ Ⓒ Ⓓ
2. Ⓐ Ⓑ Ⓒ Ⓓ   8. Ⓐ Ⓑ Ⓒ Ⓓ   14. Ⓐ Ⓑ Ⓒ Ⓓ
3. Ⓐ Ⓑ Ⓒ Ⓓ   9. Ⓐ Ⓑ Ⓒ Ⓓ   15. Ⓐ Ⓑ Ⓒ Ⓓ
4. Ⓐ Ⓑ Ⓒ Ⓓ   10. Ⓐ Ⓑ Ⓒ Ⓓ   16. Ⓐ Ⓑ Ⓒ Ⓓ
5. Ⓐ Ⓑ Ⓒ Ⓓ   11. Ⓐ Ⓑ Ⓒ Ⓓ   17. Ⓐ Ⓑ Ⓒ Ⓓ
6. Ⓐ Ⓑ Ⓒ Ⓓ   12. Ⓐ Ⓑ Ⓒ Ⓓ   18. Ⓐ Ⓑ Ⓒ Ⓓ

PRACTICE TEST V
MODULE I ANSWER KEY

1)	A
2)	B
3)	B
4)	C
5)	C
6)	D
7)	B
8)	D
9)	A
10)	D
11)	B
12)	D
13)	C
14)	B
15)	B
16)	D
17)	B
18)	0.8 or 4/5
19)	2/3
20)	146
21)	60°
22)	1

PRACTICE TEST V
MODULE I SOLUTIONS

1. 4★=2● = I.   2★=●

2▲=4● = II.   ▲=●

III. ▲★★=●●●

Correct Answer : A

2. $\dfrac{x^2y + xy^2 - xy}{x^2 + xy - x}$

$= \dfrac{xy(x+y-1)}{x(x+y-1)}$

$= \dfrac{xy}{x} = y$

Correct Answer : B

3. $9 - 5 = 4$ days

$4\sqrt{x} = 72\text{cm} - 60\text{cm}$

$4\sqrt{x} = 12\text{cm}$

$\sqrt{x} = 3\text{cm} \quad x = 9\text{cm}^2$

After 15th day's:

$= 60 + (15-5)\sqrt{9}$

$= 60 + 10\sqrt{9}$

$= 60 + 10 \cdot 3$

$= 60 + 30$

$= 90$

Correct Answer : B

4. $\dfrac{x+3}{4} - \dfrac{x}{3} = \dfrac{3}{2}$ (Find LCD)

$\dfrac{3(x+3)}{4 \cdot 3} - \dfrac{x(4)}{3(4)} = \dfrac{3(6)}{2(6)}$

$\dfrac{3x+9}{12} - \dfrac{4x}{12} = \dfrac{18}{12}$

$3x + 9 - 4x = 18$

$-x + 9 = 18$

$-x = 9$

$x = -9$

Correct Answer : C

5. Inverse Variation: y·x=k

$6 \cdot 8 = k$

$48 = k$

$yx = k$

$y \cdot 10 = 48$

$y = 4.8$

Correct Answer : C

6. From the all choices x can be D (x = 9)

$\sqrt[2]{x+16} + \sqrt[2]{x} = 8$

$\sqrt[2]{9+16} + \sqrt[2]{9} = 8$

$\sqrt[2]{25} + \sqrt[2]{9} = 8$

$5 + 3 = 8$

$8 = 8$

Correct Answer : D

PRACTICE TEST V
MODULE I SOLUTIONS

7. $-10x + 5y = -20$

$\underline{+\quad 4x - 5y = 8}$

$-6x = -12$

$x = 2$

$4(2) - 5y = 8$

$8 - 5y = 8$

$-5y = 0$

$y = 0$

Correct Answer : B

8. $= \sqrt{27} - \sqrt{81} + \sqrt{243}$

$= 3\sqrt{3} - 9 + 9\sqrt{3}$

$= 12\sqrt{3} - 9$

Correct Answer : D

9. $a = \sqrt{3}$ and $b = \sqrt{2}$, then

$\dfrac{a}{b} - \dfrac{b}{a} = \dfrac{\sqrt{3}}{\sqrt{2}} - \dfrac{\sqrt{2}}{\sqrt{3}} = \dfrac{\sqrt{3}(\sqrt{3})}{\sqrt{2}(\sqrt{3})} - \dfrac{\sqrt{2}(\sqrt{2})}{\sqrt{3}(\sqrt{2})}$

$= \dfrac{\sqrt{9}}{\sqrt{6}} - \dfrac{\sqrt{4}}{\sqrt{6}} = \dfrac{3}{\sqrt{6}} - \dfrac{2}{\sqrt{6}} = \dfrac{1}{\sqrt{6}} = \dfrac{\sqrt{6}}{6}$

Correct Answer : A

10. $f(x) = (x - 3)(x - 5)(x + 8)$

$x - 3 = 0, x = 3$

$x - 5 = 0, x = 5$

$x + 8 = 0, x = -8$

Correct Answer : D

11. $x^2 + x - 12 = 0$

$(x + 4)(x - 3) = 0$

$x = -4$ or $x = 3$ since x is positive integer x can be only 3.

$x + 3 = 3 + 3 = 6$

Correct Answer : B

12. Cosine $B = \dfrac{\text{adjacent}}{\text{hypotenuse}} = \dfrac{3}{5}$

Sine $B = \dfrac{\text{opposite}}{\text{hypotenuse}} = \dfrac{4}{5}$

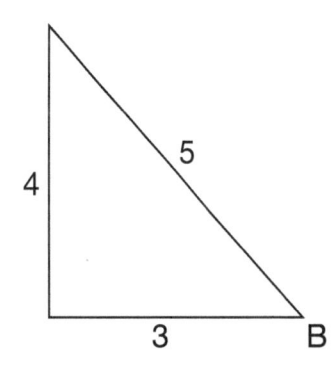

Ratio of the largest side to the shortest side

$= \dfrac{5}{3}$, or 5 to 3.

Correct Answer : D

PRACTICE TEST V
MODULE I SOLUTIONS

13.
$$\frac{x}{3} = \frac{x}{4} + 6$$
$$\frac{x}{3} - \frac{x}{4} = 6$$
$$\frac{4x}{12} - \frac{3x}{12} = 6$$
$$\frac{x}{12} = 6$$
$$x = 6 \cdot 12$$
$$x = 72$$

Correct Answer : C

14. All composite numbers: 4, 14, 21, 33

Correct Answer : B

15. 1st basket = $2x + y$
2nd basket = $y + 2z$
3rd basket = $2y + z$
$2x + y > y + 2z$ and $y + 2z > 2y + z$
$\quad x > z \quad\quad\quad\quad x > z > y$

Correct Answer : B

16. $7 + 5k = 5.5 + 10k$
$\quad k = 0.3$
Price of orange juice
$\quad y = 5.5 + 10k$
$\quad y = 5.5 + 10 \cdot (0.3)$
$\quad y = 5.5 + 3$
$\quad y = 8.5$

Correct Answer : D

17. Linear function $g(x) = mx + b$

Slope $= \frac{y_2 - y_1}{x_2 - x_1} = \frac{17 - 15}{2 - 1} = \frac{2}{1} = 2$

$g(x) = 2x + b$, use any point from the table to find b.
$15 = 2(1) + b$
$15 - 2 = b$
$b = 13$
$g(x) = 2x + 13$

Correct Answer : B

18. $4a + 5b = 16$ and $a = 3$
$4 \cdot 3 + 5b = 16$
$12 + 5b = 16$
$5b = 16 - 12$
$5b = 4$
$b = \frac{4}{5} = 0.8$

Correct Answer : 0.8 or 4/5

PRACTICE TEST V
MODULE I SOLUTIONS

19. $x^2 - 3ax - 24 = 0$, since 6 is one of the solutions of the equation that means x can be 6.

$6^2 - 3a(6) - 24 = 0$

$36 - 18a - 24 = 0$

$12 - 18a = 0$

$a = \dfrac{12}{18} = \dfrac{2}{3}$ or 2/3

Correct Answer : 2/3

20. $f(2) = 20$

$f(x) = mx^2 - 4$

$f(2) = 2^2 \cdot m - 4$

$20 = 4m - 4$

$20 + 4 = 4m$

$24 = 4m$

$6 = m$

$f(x) = 6x^2 - 4$

$f(5) = 6 \cdot 5^2 - 4$

$f(5) = 6 \cdot 25 - 4$

$f(5) = 150 - 4$

$f(5) = 146$

Correct Answer : 146

21.

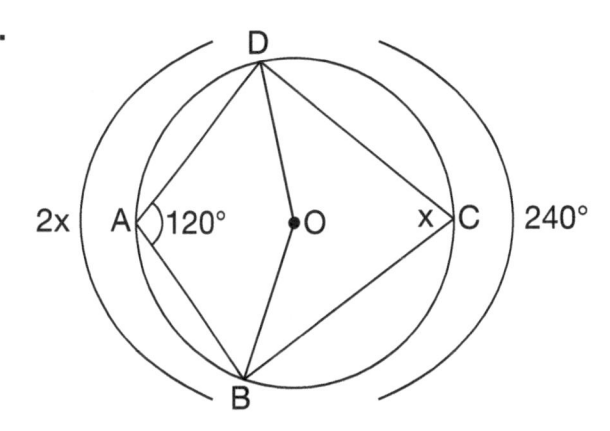

ArcBCD = 240°

ArcBCD = 2x

2x + 240° = 360°

2x = 120°

x = 60°

Correct Answer : 60°

22. If P(x) is divisible by x+1, then x + 1 = 0, x = −1

$P(-1) = (-1)^{2018} + (-1)^{2019} + (-1)^{2020}$

$P(-1) = 1 - 1 + 1$

$P(-1) = 1$

Correct Answer : 1

125

PRACTICE TEST V
MODULE II ANSWER KEY

1)	D
2)	C
3)	C
4)	D
5)	B
6)	B
7)	A
8)	B
9)	C
10)	A
11)	A

12)	B
13)	D
14)	B
15)	A
16)	B
17)	A
18)	B
19)	1
20)	15
21)	11
22)	18

PRACTICE TEST V
MODULE II SOLUTIONS

1. $f(x) = x^3 + 6x^2 + 9x$

$x^3 + 6x^2 + 9x = 0$

$x(x^2 + 6x + 9) = 0$

$x(x+3)^2 = 0$

$x = 0$ or $x = -3$

Correct Answer : D

2. $x - 2\sqrt{x} - 3 = 0$

$x - 3 = (2\sqrt{x})^2$

$(x-3)^2 = (\sqrt{4x})^2$

$(x-3)^2 = 4x$

$x^2 - 6x + 9 = 4x$

$x^2 - 6x - 4x + 9 = 0$

$x^2 - 10x + 9 = 0$

$(x-9) \cdot (x-1) = 0$

$x = 9$ or $x = 1$ (x cannot be 1)

$\dfrac{x}{x-1} = \dfrac{9}{8}$

Correct Answer : C

3. The sum of five consecutive positive integers are: $x + x + 1 + x + 2 + x + 3 + x + 4 = 75$

$5x + 10 = 75$

$5x = 65$

$x = 13$

Greatest one: $x + 4 = 13 + 4 = 17$

Correct Answer : C

4. If the ratio of $\dfrac{1}{3} : \dfrac{1}{b}$ is equal to $\dfrac{1}{18} : \dfrac{1}{12}$

$\dfrac{1}{3} \cdot \dfrac{b}{1} = \dfrac{1}{18} \cdot \dfrac{12}{1}$

$\dfrac{b}{3} = \dfrac{12}{18}$

$b = \dfrac{3 \cdot 12}{18}$

$b = 2$

Correct Answer : D

5. $3^{2x-4} = 27^{x-6}$

$3^{2x-4} = 3^{3x-18}$

$2x - 4 = 3x - 18$

$-4 + 18 = 3x - 2x$

$14 = x$

Correct Answer : B

127

PRACTICE TEST V
MODULE II SOLUTIONS

6. $\dfrac{1}{\dfrac{1}{x+3}+\dfrac{1}{x+5}} =$

$\dfrac{1}{\dfrac{(x+5)}{(x+3)\cdot(x+5)}+\dfrac{(x+3)}{(x+5)\cdot(x+3)}} =$

$\dfrac{1}{\dfrac{2x+8}{x^2+5x+3x+15}} = \dfrac{x^2+8x+15}{2x+8}$

Correct Answer : B

7. $\left(\dfrac{1+i}{1-i}\right)^{2020} = \left(\dfrac{(1+i)(1+i)}{(1-i)(1+i)}\right)^{2020} = \left(\dfrac{2i}{2}\right)^{2020}$

$(i)^{2020} = (i^2)^{1010} = (-1)^{1010} = 1$

Correct Answer : A

8. Tea $= \dfrac{25-20}{20} = \dfrac{5}{20} = 25\%$

Coffee $= \dfrac{18-12}{12} = \dfrac{6}{12} = 50\%$

Soda $= \dfrac{24-20}{20} = \dfrac{4}{20} = 20\%$

Water $= \dfrac{120-90}{90} = \dfrac{30}{90} \approx 33\%$

the highest rate of profit is Coffee.

Correct Answer : B

9. $(2\Phi1) = \dfrac{2^2+1}{4} = \dfrac{5}{4}$

$(3\Phi1) = \dfrac{3^2+1}{4} = \dfrac{10}{4}$

$\left(\dfrac{5}{4}\oplus\dfrac{10}{4}\right) = \dfrac{3\cdot\dfrac{5}{4}\cdot\dfrac{10}{4}}{5} = \dfrac{15\cancel{0}}{8\cancel{0}} = \dfrac{15}{8}$

Correct Answer : C

10. Let $a = 2k, b = 4k, c = 6k$

$\dfrac{1}{8k^3}+\dfrac{1}{27k^3}+\dfrac{1}{216k^3} = \dfrac{1}{6}$

$\dfrac{27}{216k^3}+\dfrac{8}{216k^3}+\dfrac{1}{216k^3} = \dfrac{1}{6}$

$216k^3 = 6\cdot 36$

$216k^3 = 216$

$k^3 = 1$

$k = 1$

$V_c = 216k^3 = 216$

Correct Answer : A

11. Percent of the graph represents the car transportation: $\dfrac{60}{200} = \dfrac{6}{20}$

$= \dfrac{6\cdot 5}{20\cdot 5} = \dfrac{30}{100} = 30\%$

Correct Answer : A

PRACTICE TEST V
MODULE II SOLUTIONS

12. $2^{4a} = \dfrac{32}{2^a}$

$2^{5a} = 2^5, a = 1$

Correct Answer : B

13. $\dfrac{1}{4} > -3$, then $\dfrac{-(-3)}{3} = 1$

$(-4) \triangle 1 \implies -4 \leq 1$

$1^2 - (-4) = 5$

Correct Answer : D

14. $2k^2 - 3k + 1 = 0$

$(2k - 1)(k - 1) = 0$

$k = 1$ or $k = \dfrac{1}{2}$

Correct Answer : B

15. (2, 3) and (−2, 7).

Slope of line K = $\dfrac{y_2 - y_1}{x_2 - x_1} = \dfrac{7-3}{-2-2} = -\dfrac{4}{4} = 1$,

since line K and line L are perpendicular slope of L is 1.

$y = mx + b$, $y = x + b$

use (3, 1) to find b.

$1 = 3(1) + b$

$-2 = b$

$y = x - 2$

Correct Answer : B

16. $3y = 6 + 4x$ and $y = 8 - 2x$, then $3(8 - 2x) = 6 + 4x$.

$24 - 6x = 6 + 4x$

$24 - 6 = 4x + 6x$

$18 = 10x$

$1.8 = x$

$4.4 = y$

Correct Answer : B

17.

If $6x = 8y + 10$ and $x - 3y = -5$, then $x = 3y - 5$.

$6(3y-5) = 8y + 10$

$18y - 30 = 8y + 10$

$18y - 8y = 30 + 10$

$10y = 40$

$y = 4$, then $\dfrac{y}{2} = \dfrac{4}{2} = 2$

Correct Answer : A

18. $\dfrac{6}{8} < \dfrac{x}{2} - \dfrac{2y}{4} < \dfrac{3}{2}$

$= \dfrac{6}{8} < \dfrac{4x}{8} - \dfrac{4y}{8} < \dfrac{12}{8}$

$6 < 4x - 4y < 12$

$\dfrac{6}{4} < x - y < \dfrac{12}{4}$

$\dfrac{3}{2} < x - y < 3$

One possible value of x − y is 2.

Correct Answer : B

PRACTICE TEST V
MODULE II SOLUTIONS

19. $\dfrac{2a-3-4a+8}{a-2} = \dfrac{3}{a-2}$

$-2a+5 = 3$

$-2a = -2$

$a = 1$

Correct Answer : A

20. $x^2 + 2x - 15 = (x-a)(x+b)$

$x^2 + 2x - 15 = x^2 + x(b-a) - ab$

$-15 = -ab$, then $ab = 15$

Correct Answer : B

21. $x^2 + 12x - 13 = 0$

$(x+13)(x-1) = 0$

$x = -13$ and $x = 1$, since x is a positive integer x can be only 1.

$x + 10 = 10 + 1 = 11$

Correct Answer : 11

22. $6x - ay + 12 = 0$

$y = \dfrac{6x}{a} + \dfrac{12}{a}$, slope $= \dfrac{6}{a}$

$\dfrac{6}{a} = \dfrac{1}{3}$, $a = 18$

Correct Answer : 18